THE
Mindfulness
COOKBOOK

THE
Mindfulness
COOKBOOK

EAT IN THE "NOW"
AND BE YOUR PERFECT
WEIGHT FOR LIFE

Dr. Patrizia Collard & Helen Stephenson

hamlyn

An Hachette UK Company
www.hachette.co.uk

First published in Great Britain in 2015 by
Hamlyn, a division of Octopus Publishing Group Ltd
Carmelite House
50 Victoria Embankment
London EC4Y 0DZ
www.octopusbooks.co.uk
www.octopusbooksusa.com

Distributed in the US by
Hachette Book Group
1290 Avenue of the Americas
4th and 5th Floors
New York, NY 10020

Distributed in Canada by
Canadian Manda Group
664 Annette St.
Toronto, Ontario, Canada M6S 2C8

ISBN 978 0600 632 61 0

Printed and bound in China

10 9 8 7 6 5 4 3 2 1

Contents

Introduction

How often do we think about food, or the effect food has on our bodies? We are living in a culture that is obsessed with the young, the good-looking, and the slim. Most of us, to a greater or lesser degree, are unhappy with the way we look and whether we relate that to our eating habits or not, we think about food many times during the day.

Definition of mindfulness

Mindfulness lies at the core of Buddhist meditative practices but it is universal. It can be described as a way of being, a way of seeing, and a way of connecting to your senses.

> **"The present is the only time that any of us have to be alive, to know anything, to perceive, to learn, to act, to change, to heal."**
>
> **JON KABAT-ZINN**

Staying in touch with the present in a mindful way from one moment to the next may lead to you experiencing life differently. You may become a little less stuck in your ways, perceiving more options, and finding more strength, more balance, more understanding, and confidence. The practice of mindfulness can diffuse our negativity, aggression, and unstable emotions.

Mindfulness has also been described as "bare attention." That term was coined by German-born Buddhist monk N Thera, one of the great figures of 20th-century Buddhism. It is called "bare" because it attends just to the bare facts of perception as presented, either through the five senses or through the mind, without reacting to them or judging them. We behave rather like an outside observer, perceiving what is happening to us, accepting, and allowing it. The thoughts or feelings we observe are not us, they are just something that is happening to us.

The fusion of mindfulness-based stress reduction (MBSR) and mindfulness-based cognitive therapy (MBCT)

Research estimates that around 20 percent of the population in Western countries will suffer an episode of clinical depression at least once in their lifetime. However, up until the 1990s, CBT (cognitive behavioral therapy) research did not explore the fact that patients who have had more than one or two episodes of depression are susceptible to becoming depressed again and again. Very little hard data focused on this phenomenon of "relapse" until researchers began to look for a more cost- and time-effective intervention to deal with it. Regular CBT would be used for acute depression and the "new approach" of MBSR would hopefully cater for relapse prevention.

HOW MBCT WORKS
- Identify your cognitive "distortions"—conscious awareness.
- Identify the fact that the imagined "threat" is only a thought.
- Sit with what "is"—I am okay, even now.
- Appraise your internal resources—"I can."

Mindfulness-based cognitive therapy is an integration of mindfulness-based stress reduction with cognitive behavioral therapy. In conventional CBT, the focus is on changing unhelpful beliefs. In MBCT, the focus is rather on methodical training to be more aware, moment by moment, of physical sensations and of thoughts and feelings as mental events. Research on MBCT shows that it can halve the relapse rate in recovered patients who have had three or more episodes of depression. Other targeted versions of MBCT have now been developed, including MBCT for chronic-fatigue syndrome, for oncology patients, in schools, for anxiety disorders, and in the treatment of trauma, to mention just a few. Mindfulness-based eating interventions are being developed as we speak.

What is mindful eating?

By bringing mindfulness into your life, more specifically into your eating life, you will learn to stop, to tune in, and to listen. You will become interested in what is really important to you. Through the various practices in this book, you make time and pay attention to what is going on in your life right now. You will come to understand how your thoughts and feelings, if unnoticed, can pull you away from the present moment, and make you go for the chocolate to avoid the discomfort of feeling upset or lonely.

When we pay attention to our food intake, we have to face our true longings and explore what we really want. By not being mindful with our "true" hunger, we tend to eat more, when having less could be what is needed. By becoming mindful we develop understanding, and in this process we become more forgiving and kinder to ourselves. Just by reading this book you can start to replace hating your body with appreciating your inner wisdom. You can release yourself from the grip of shame and anger and replace it with understanding. You will become less obsessed about food and how you look and more attuned to the appreciation of being alive.

Reading this book, and practicing the exercises, will help you to:

- *reconnect* with your body and its senses
- *retrain* yourself to enjoy your food without guilt or shame
- *feel full* and eat less as you learn to feel truly nourished
- *break free* from destructive eating habits
- *become aware* of the feelings and thoughts that keep your unhelpful eating patterns in place
- *reconnect* with your own inner wisdom
- *live life* with zest and creativity
- *free yourself* from negative thinking and develop compassion and kindness.

Factors that influence our eating habits

The genetic code

It is obvious that some people have a larger frame than others, but holding onto the idea that our weight is dictated solely by genetics assumes that change is impossible. Mindful eating invites us to accept the fact that we cannot change the basic frame of our bodies, but that we can still find our own ideal weight, together with a healthy sense of appreciation and respect for our bodies.

Reward and punishment

There are countless times when we have eaten something unhealthy (and delicious) because "we are worth it"; and times when we have felt obliged to eat something that we don't like. We may assume it's normal to live with this inner struggle of "I must" and "I mustn't." By becoming a witness to the feelings, a space is created around them and we are no longer a hostage to them.

The teenage years

Being a teenager is a time of constant changes in the body and a time when we become self-conscious about our size and eating habits. Views are formed about how we see ourselves and how others see us. But now it is important to acknowledge that whatever it was happened in the past. Mindfulness enables us to let go of those stories and feelings, and to replace them with what is needed now.

Emotions

Very few people in the West eat out of hunger alone. Most of us eat from a place of emotion. We often do things, such as eating chocolate while watching TV, without being conscious of the thoughts and feelings that drive the behavior. We live and eat on autopilot, reacting to signals from the brain or cravings from the mind. Mindfulness is about having the awareness to see the formation of the emotion, to see its origins, and with practice, even to see the very first thought that started it all.

Lack of exercise

We live in a sedentary world. Products are consistently delivered, enabling us to be less active. The voices of the medical profession are drowned out by the noises that encourage us to do less and eat more. Research suggests that walking every day for at least 15 minutes is an important factor in improving health. Exercise is one of our best supports in achieving our ideal weight, size, and shape.

Addictions

We experience the strength of addiction when we feel forced to eat the chocolate, when we are desperate to open that package, and when we experience a feeling of no choice, of inevitability.

The food industry exists to sell food, and making us go back for more is what the product is designed to do. By recognizing this fact, we are released from feelings of failure and weakness, and with mindfulness we will be able to break this cycle.

Alcohol

Alcohol creates a mind that is open to suggestion and more willing to throw away caution, and is responsible for a lot of bad food choices. Alcohol really has the potential to derail any attempts to change your shape or weight. It is one of the most concentrated sources of calories with little nutritional value. If you want to become more mindful around food, moderating alcohol consumption is a must.

Social pressure

Eating with others is wonderful but we may make choices that we would never make if we were eating alone, and we eat with only a fraction of the awareness that we might usually feel. Knowing this helps you to approach those situations calmly, and by being clear about the choices you have, you can act in accordance with your values and wishes.

Laziness

Even the most efficient and focused person will occasionally think, "I can't be bothered to cook tonight." This is where mindfulness comes into play: seeing the feeling and not identifying with it, and so separating it from yourself, will help you to respond with calm. Then you will be more likely to make a healthy choice, instead of simply following the usual habitual patterns.

Sleep

When people are sleeping less, the accumulation of body fat appears to increase—by up to 32 percent. Also, when people suffer from daytime sleepiness, they are far more likely to crave high-sugar foodstuff. Mindfulness in general might help us to sleep better and to make the positive choices that will help us to avoid weight gain.

Stress

During stress, the mind is on reaction mode as opposed to responding mode. The stress hormone cortisol interferes with the digestion of food, can lead to food cravings, and plays a significant part in people putting on weight. It speeds up the accumulation of fat around the waistline, while at the same time breaking down highly prized lean muscle. Mindfulness practices have been shown to trigger the "relaxation response," a series of physical reactions that are associated with a greater feeling of comfort and ease.

10 steps to mindful eating

1 Listen to your body
Before you pile a mountain of food on your plate or break open a family-size bag of potato chips, take a moment to listen to your physical needs. Are you hungry? If you are, how hungry are you? Serve up just enough food to satisfy the hunger of the body, rather than trying to quench the limitless desire of the mind. You'll be much less likely to go back for more than if you simply had the bag of potato chips sitting on your lap.

2 Use smaller serving plates and bowls
Studies have shown that our satisfaction is tied in to "relative" portion sizes. So, if we have a very small plate that is piled high with food, we will feel much more satisfied than if we have a large plate with a small amount of food—even if the large serving on the small plate contains less! Some new tableware could be the best investment you ever made.

3 Be flexible when eating out
Restaurant menus are generally written in a way that encourages you to eat as much as possible (and why wouldn't they be?) but you don't have to play that game. There is no obligation to have an appetizer, entrée, and dessert. Why not have an appetizer instead of an entrée? Why not have tea or coffee instead of a dessert for a change? Oh, and don't be afraid to ask for excess food to be put in a doggie-bag.

4 Serve up at source
When serving food at home, try to plate it up by the oven or stove, rather than at the table. If the excess is on the table in front of you while you are eating, then that's where your mind is likely to be.

Studies have shown that you are likely to eat faster with the excess in front of you. Presumably this is prompted by some survival instinct from the past, when we weren't sure where the next meal was coming from.

5 When you eat, just eat
Portion sizes are intimately related to "how" we eat. For example, if you sit down at a table with a large box of chocolates and no distractions, you are unlikely to polish off the entire box. This is partly because you would be more aware of hunger levels, but also because you would probably feel greedy, embarrassed, or ashamed. But when you're watching TV, surfing the net, or involved in some other activity, this awareness can be drowned out.

6 Learn what a portion size is
If you want to become more mindful of portion sizes, and possibly even to follow the recommended quantities with certain foods, it can be really useful to know and understand what portion sizes are (quite different from "serving sizes," incidentally, which can be frighteningly large). As a general rule, a "cup" is about the size of a large tennis ball, 3 oz of meat comprises the size of a deck of cards, and 1 oz cheese is about the size of a domino. This may help you to avoid having to weigh everything.

7 Think little and often
Many people overeat at meals because they are worried they might feel hungry later on. The body doesn't really work like this and all overeating tends to do is increase the dramatic swings in blood-sugar levels that will, in all likelihood, have you reaching for the cookie tin. Try to maintain a stable blood-sugar level and moderate level of satiety by eating small meals throughout the day, rather than just a couple of ridiculously large meals.

8 Have a salad as an appetizer
We often dive into large portions of rich and color-dense foods simply because we're hungry. The truth is, in these situations, we're often so hungry that we'd eat just about anything. So be smart and eat some raw vegetables or salad to burn off that extreme hunger before the meal itself. That way you will not feel the same need to overindulge in richer-tasting foods.

9 Have a glass of water before eating
The sensation of thirst is often confused with the feeling of hunger, so that whenever we feel thirsty, we tend to reach out for a snack, or, if about to serve up a meal, we're likely to put more food on the plate. To ensure that you are listening to the right signals, sip a good-size glass of water in the ten to fifteen minutes leading up to a meal. This way you can be sure that you are serving up only what the body actually needs.

10 Shop smart
Bulk-buying foods can often enable you to pick up some great bargains, but you know your own mind. If you are unable or unwilling to break those down into smaller portion sizes when you get home, then consider the possibility of buying smaller versions. While you may not get the same value for money, take a moment to think of the cost (financial, physical, mental, and emotional) of overeating large portions of food.

Frequently used practices

Once we start to engage in a friendly relationship with our bodies, the first foundation of mindfulness, our lives become lighter and more joyful, easy and relaxed. There is no need to fight our body or treat it as an enemy—better to start with a feeling of wonder that you have this body, and that it sustains you day and night. When you are able to accept the body, to respect and love it, you will not only become grateful to be in this body but you will become grateful for all existence.

The body scan

The key objective in doing the body scan is to enhance awareness of physiological sensations and to train your mind to stay focused over a longer than usual period of time on a particular task in the now.

Practice for around forty minutes six times per week, with no expectation or judgment of a particular outcome. Let go of ideas such as success, failure, and relaxation, and bring an open mind, curiosity, and a sense of adventure to the practice. Lie down on a mat or bed, or sit upright on a chair, and focus for a while on the movement of the breath before directing attention to each region of the body and observing what happens when doing this. Each body scan is a new beginning, a new "NOW."

The body scan consists of three steps:
- Intentionally moving the attention to a selected area
- Holding the awareness there and experiencing the sensations
- Moving on.

By regularly practicing the body scan you will make some good discoveries:

PAYING ATTENTION is a good practice. Most of us find it relatively easy to focus on our bodies. By paying attention to your body, you make it "happy" as you trigger its relaxation response.

IT HELPS YOU to reconnect with your body and understand its language.

IT IS A GOOD WAY to be nice to yourself. Remember you are your own best friend. By turning to your body, you are nourishing yourself. You are appreciating it as it is right now, acknowledging that the body serves us day in day out, and sustains us in the best possible way. It is our home!

WHEN YOU START to practice body scan, do it in the morning. Normally, when we wake up our minds are not yet busy, so it is easier to focus. Of course, you should choose the time that is best for you—some of us are larks and others are owls.

Here is a brief description of the actual exercise:

TAKE A FEW MOMENTS to get in touch with the movement of your breath and the sensations in your body. Remind yourself of the intention of this practice. Its aim is not to feel any different, relaxed, or calm—this may happen or it may not. Instead, the intention of the practice is, as best you can, to bring awareness to any sensations you detect as you focus your attention on each part of the body in turn.

NOW BRING THE FOCUS of your awareness down the left leg, into the left foot. Focus on each of the toes of the left foot in turn, bringing a gentle curiosity to investigating the quality of sensations you find. When you are ready, on an in-breath, feel or imagine the breath entering the lungs, and then passing down into the abdomen, into the left leg, the left foot, and out to the toes of the left foot. Then, on the out-breath, feel or imagine the breath coming all the way back up, out of the foot, into the leg up through the abdomen, chest, and out through the nose. Just practice this "breathing into" as best you can, approaching it playfully.

NEXT ALLOW YOUR AWARENESS to expand into the rest of the foot, then to the ankle, the top of the foot, and right into the bones and joints. Move your awareness to the lower left leg—the calf, shin, and knee in turn.

CONTINUE TO BRING AWARENESS, and a gentle curiosity, to the physical sensations in each part of the rest of the body in turn—to the upper left leg, the right toes, right foot, right leg, pelvic area, back, abdomen, chest, fingers, hands, arms, shoulder, neck, head, and face. In each area, as best as you can, bring the same detailed level of awareness and gentle curiosity to the bodily sensations present. As you leave each major area, breathe into it on the in-breath, and let go of that region on the out-breath.

WHEN YOU BECOME AWARE of tension, or other intense sensations, in a particular part of the body, you can breathe into that region, using the in-breath gently to bring awareness right into the tension, and, as best as you can, have a sense of letting go, or releasing, on the out-breath.

THE MIND WILL WANDER away from the breath and the body from time to time. That is entirely normal. It is what minds do. When you notice it, acknowledge it, noticing where the mind has gone off to, and then gently return your attention to the body scan.

After you have scanned the whole body in this way, spend a few minutes being aware of the body as a whole, and of the breath flowing freely in and out.

Walking meditation

Walking can be a form of meditation in action, eyes open. The experience of walking is our focus. We are not withdrawing our attention from the outside world to the same extent that we do for the mindfulness of breathing or body-scan practices. Naturally, we have to be aware of obstacles outside of ourselves, and other people. Out of doors, we will be aware of many other things, too—wind, sun, rain, and the sounds of nature, humans, and machines. One of the biggest differences between sitting inside to meditate and walking outside is that it's easier, for most people, to be more intensely and more easily aware of their bodies while doing walking meditation. When your body is in motion, it is generally easier to be aware of it compared to when you are sitting still. This can make walking meditation a powerful experience, both in becoming aware of your body and in finding profound enjoyment from the practice.

The form of walking meditation described here is best done out of doors. For your first attempt, you might want to find a park or open space where you will be able to walk for 20 minutes without encountering traffic.

• Note your standing posture and the touch sensations of your feet. Let your arms hang naturally.

• As you start walking, keep your attention on the sole of the foot, rather than any other body part. Initially, just notice how you lift, push, and drop your foot.

• Thoughts not related to this experience may come up, but just let them go into the background and focus on experiencing walking—notice perhaps how your whole body shifts and adapts with every step.

• If your thoughts become too active, gently let them go, and reconnect with focusing on walking.

Breath–body–thoughts exercise

Our minds sometimes create their own interpretation of events, and this affects our reaction to them. Facts + self-deprecating thoughts = depressive interpretation of events (internal propaganda). Once a negative interpretation stream is started, contrary information is ignored and consistent information is noticed. Therapists used to think that these thoughts were caused by depression. Cognitive therapy teaches the opposite. Negative interpretation causes reduced self-esteem, increased guilt, interrupted concentration, and undermined social interaction, plus, possibly, biological effects (stress-response).

• Catch negative thoughts and treat them as hypothesis, not fact. Then seek ways to disprove the hypothesis (reality testing). In this way, we learn to recognize thoughts as thoughts and not as facts.

• Allow thoughts to enter, see how they make you feel/how you interpret them, and then bring your thoughts back to neutrality. Awareness!

• Take a few moments now to become aware of the thoughts that are arising in your mind. Imagine yourself sitting in a movie theater, watching an empty screen, just waiting for thoughts to come. When they come, can you see what exactly they are and what happens to them? Some of them will vanish as you become aware of them.

• Focus on specific body reactions and the feelings arising from negative thoughts, such as tension or anger. Observe and stand next to emotion, but do not be dragged down by it.

Everyday informal practices

Every day, remember to do at least one activity mindfully. Here are some examples.

• When you brush your teeth, notice the sensations of the brush on each tooth. Are you thinking about the day or night ahead of you? Notice this and bring your attention back to brushing your teeth.

• In the shower, instead of writing lists in your head or planning a speech for the lunchtime meeting, really feel the water touching your body and be aware of its temperature. Smell the soap or shower gel, notice what it feels like on your skin and feel your muscles relaxing. Then feel gratitude for the luxury of having water just for washing.

• When you hear a sound, any sound—a phone ringing, a passing car, an airplane above, a bird singing, a dog barking—kindly remember to embrace this moment and engage for a few minutes in mindful breathing and listening.

The raisin practice

The "Raisin Experience" was first introduced to the public by Jon Kabat–Zinn, a professor at the University of Massachusetts. This basic practice aims to show us two things:

1. Perception influences taste
2. Heightened awareness can provide us with a richer and more satisfying eating experience.

In the raisin practice you are invited to eat one raisin mindfully, slowly, and with awareness of the use of all your senses. Participants often comment on the eye-opening effect this practice can have in relation to their eating patterns. Typical comments are:

"I noticed that no one raisin looks the same in color, shape, and with its ridges."

"I had a much more pleasurable experience, because the practice of mindfully eating it gave me a heightened sense of its taste, color, and texture."

"I noticed how much more satisfaction I get out of eating one raisin mindfully compared to my normal habit of eating them one handful at a time."

"I noticed how often I eat mindlessly, because my mind was all over the place rather than focusing on the food in front of me."

"I was surprised how it brought back memories from my time as a child with my family, as if it was yesterday."

"I was surprised how my sense of time changed. Normally I get easily bored, but I was so absorbed in the practice, that I didn't notice the time at all."

Beforehand

Try to avoid all possible distractions for the time of the practice, such as cell phones, tablets, reading the newspaper, etc.

Sit and ground yourself by feeling your feet on the floor, your buttocks on the seat. Feel your entire posture. Do you feel tight or loose, collapsed or upright, tired or agitated?

- Connect with your breathing.
- Ask yourself if you are hungry or just fancy a bite to eat.
- Are your thoughts/emotions encouraging you to eat something now?
- Are any of your senses, such as smell or sight, triggering your wish to eat?

Practice

Now look at what's on your plate and imagine that you are seeing it for the first time ever. You could imagine that you are coming from another part of this world, or even from another planet, or you are a small child. This may feel a bit ridiculous, but it is helpful if, for this moment, you try to perceive the items on your plate as if you have never seen them before.

LOOK AT THE COLORS, the different textures, the forms, and the size. Do you see any patterns? If you hold an item of food, either with flatware or your hands, and turn it around, does it look different from different angles? Is the light reflected differently, showing you light and darker areas? Are there details you didn't notice before?

IF YOU CAN TOUCH IT (raw food, bread, fruits, vegetables, snacks) what do you feel? Is it hard, soft, rough, smooth, wet, dry, sticky, hot, cool, heavy, light? Does it feel the same all over, or are there differences between different parts of it? How do you hold the food? Gently or with tight pressure? Did you notice that your body knows how to pick up food and hold it, without you interfering?

SMELL IT by moving it to your nose. Does it smell sweet, sour, bitter, salty, or kind of meaty? Is the smell strong or subtle, or overpowering? Have any memories, associations, or images occurred during this part of the practice?

WHEN YOU ARE READY, and when you are willing to do so, put the food into your mouth. You can even place it on your lips to see how that feels. Did you notice the movement of the joints of your hand and arm, and the coordination necessary to bring the food to your mouth? But please, don't chew it yet. Once more feel its texture, weight, and taste, and experience how your tongue is moving it. Has the smell intensified? Is the texture changing? What about the taste?

AFTER MOVING it around with your tongue, and when you are ready, start to chew it. Does it make a sound? Does the chewing change the food's texture, taste, and moisture? Don't count your bites, let the body chew and let the body decide when to swallow. Does it go down in one big gulp or do you need to swallow several times? Who made the decision to swallow? Your body or you?

THIRTY MINUTES to an hour after the meal, ask yourself: "How do I feel now?" Are you still hungry or are you satisfied? Are you very full, heavy, or light, tired, or energized? Knowing this could help you to make better choices next time around.

Getting started—
A sensory recipe experience

Guided practice—Thai veg salad

All five senses are involved in wanting food, and enjoying it—taste, smell, sight, sound, and touch. They work together to give us a complete sensory experience, enabling us to savor our food.

Simply thinking of food can make you hungry. The following recipe will introduce you to the process of mindful eating, focusing on each sense to guide you through the basic principles.

1 This recipe is simple and will take just ten minutes to cook plus cooling time. It is full of bright and colorful ingredients to awaken the sense of sight, a wide variety of textures to explore, aromatic herbs, and most importantly, it has a fantastic, fresh taste. Take time to display and garnish the food so it looks appetizing—a dish you are proud of having prepared. Enjoy the exotic brightness and interesting layers.

2 When making the dressing, take the time to sample the flavors—the sourness of the lime and the saltiness of the soy sauce, for example. Remember to use as many of your senses as possible. As the ingredients warm, smell the sweet comforting marmalade and spicy chile.

3 Really look at the salad ingredients while you are preparing them. Notice texture and color. What does the food feel like? Is it hard or soft? Grainy or sticky? Moist or dry? Enjoy the sound and sensation of chopping different shapes and surfaces. Crush a herb leaf in your fingers. Does that release the aroma? How do the scallions contrast with the sweet, peppery mango?

4 As you toss the salad in the dressing, notice how the ingredients combine to make a different set of textures and smells.

5 Take small mouthfuls and at least two minutes to finish each one. Chew as slowly as possible to give yourself time to experience each sensation. Close your eyes and concentrate on the smell, the taste, and the texture.

6 Notice the peanuts, the way they crunch and crumble in your mouth. How does the saltiness of the soy sauce bring out the sweet flavor burst of a cherry tomato? What is your favorite ingredient? Do you like the chile kick or the freshness of the Lebanese cucumber? Notice if the intensity of the flavors change, and concentrate on the sensation of swallowing.

Thai veg salad

Calories per serving 180
Serves 4
Preparation time 10 minutes,
    plus cooling
Cooking time 2 minutes

8 oz cherry tomatoes, quartered
1 Lebanese cucumber, thinly sliced
1 green papaya or green mango
1 large red chile, seeded and
    thinly sliced
1½ cups bean sprouts
4 scallions, thinly sliced
small handful of Thai basil leaves
small handful of mint leaves
small handful of fresh cilantro leaves
4 tablespoons unsalted peanuts,
    coarsely chopped

Chili dressing
2 tablespoons sweet chili sauce
2 tablespoons light soy sauce
2 tablespoons lime juice
2 tablespoons lime marmalade,
    warmed

Make the dressing. Put all the ingredients in a small saucepan and warm over low heat, stirring, until combined. Let cool.

Put the tomatoes, cucumber, papaya or mango, chile, bean sprouts, scallions, and herbs in a bowl. Add the dressing and toss well. Transfer to a platter. Sprinkle over the peanuts and serve immediately.

Smell

Our sense of smell is more closely related to how things taste than any other sense; 75 percent of what we perceive as taste comes from our sense of smell. When we say a meal tasted good, we might not know that a great part of this is due to our experience of its smell.

When we put food in our mouths, odor molecules from the food travel to olfactory receptor cells at the top of the nasal cavity, which sits just beneath the brain. The olfactory bulb is part of the brain's limbic system, also called the emotional brain. The olfactory bulb has access to the amygdala, which processes emotion, and the hippocampus, which is responsible for associative learning. When we have a cold, we can't taste much. This is due to the build-up of mucus in the nasal passage preventing the odor molecules from reaching the olfactory receptor cells. The brain receives no signal and we experience the food as tasteless. Thus when the sense of smell doesn't work, the sense of taste is not triggered. When children are made to eat food or take medicine they don't like, or that tastes bitter, they hold their nose and gulp it down fast to avoid tasting it.

Smell can bring back a flood of memories and has a very powerful effect on mood and emotion. Our emotional repertoire can remind us of characteristic smells associated with places and activities in the past. For example, the smell of strong disinfectant can remind you of hospital visits you made as a child. If you encounter that smell later in life, it can trigger feelings of loneliness and abandonment.

Explore smell *Lemon & cardamom madeleines*

Calories per serving 80

Makes about 30

Preparation time 20 minutes,
   plus setting

Cooking time 30 minutes

9 tablespoons lightly salted butter,
   melted, plus extra for greasing

1 cup all-purpose flour,
   plus extra for dusting

2 teaspoons cardamom pods

3 eggs

$2/3$ cup superfine sugar

finely grated zest of 1 lemon

1½ teaspoons baking powder

Glaze

2 tablespoons lemon juice

¾ cup sifted confectioners' sugar,
   plus extra for dusting

AWARENESS POINTS

- Cardamom seeds are intensely aromatic when crushed. Green pods are sweet flavored and are used in making Garam Masala Chai. Black pods have a smokier aroma.

- Notice the fresh, zingy smell of the lemon before and after you grate the rind.

- The smell of baking is one of the most comforting and appetizing. Use the half-hour baking time to savor positive feelings.

Grease a madeleine tray with melted butter and dust with flour. Tap out the excess flour.

Crush the cardamom pods using a mortar and pestle to release the seeds. Remove the shells and crush the seeds a little further.

Put the eggs, superfine sugar, lemon zest, and crushed cardamom seeds in a heatproof bowl and rest the bowl over a saucepan of gently simmering water. Whisk with a handheld electric whisk until the mixture is thick and pale and the mixture leaves a trail when lifted.

Sift the flour and baking powder into the bowl and gently fold in using a large metal spoon. Drizzle the melted butter around the edges of the mixture and fold the ingredients together to combine. Spoon the batter into the madeleine sections until about two-thirds full. (Keep the remaining batter for a second batch.)

Bake in a preheated oven, 425°F, for about 10 minutes until risen and golden. Leave in the tray for 5 minutes, then transfer to a wire rack.

Make the glaze by putting the lemon juice in a bowl and beating in the confectioners' sugar. Brush over the madeleines and set. Serve dusted with confectioners' sugar.

Sight

Sight is a trigger for appetite and does not affect the ability to taste, although it influences our perception of taste. For example, some studies show that a darker color makes us think a drink is stronger. When food looks fresh and is well presented, it triggers our taste buds and saliva glands. A well-presented buffet leads us to anticipate a tasty meal. If the buffet looks drab, the salad is limp, and the food is colorless, we are less inclined to have positive expectations.

The main reason for sight's influence is memory of past experiences with color and flavor. We remember what fresh bread looks like compared with moldy bread. We can identify vegetables and fruits that are fresh, those that are past their best, and those that are unripe. We go for the yellow banana, not the green. We choose the brown/green apple for sour taste, the red apple for sweet taste.

TIP

If the chocolate bar or potato chip bag is left on the coffee table in front of the TV, chances are you won't resist. Put it away and replace it with some healthier options, such as carrot sticks, or apples and grapes with cheese. Remember, out of sight is out of mind. Put healthy food in a prime position; ideally, unhealthy food should be hidden.

Memory influences our food choices. If we have had a good experience with certain food, we think it looks good. If we have no experience with it, our minds will try to associate it with something familiar. We might avoid a specific food because we don't recognize it and it looks strange, weird even, and not very appetizing. We might think we know how it tastes just by looking at it. But we might be mistaken.

If you are hungry, the mind recognizes the overriding need for food and makes you select something, even if it doesn't look that enticing. So try something that looks unfamiliar to you. You might feel better because you stepped out of autopilot, happier, and empowered. Feeling happier means you can make better choices.

Explore sight *Tomato & mozzarella salad*

Calories per serving 212
Serves 4
Preparation time 15 minutes

1 lb ripe tomatoes, preferably different
    types, such as heirloom
    and cherry and plum
about 3 tablespoons olive oil
2 tablespoons aged balsamic vinegar
small handful of basil leaves
5 oz mini mozzarella balls
salt and pepper

Cut half the tomatoes into thick slices and the other half into wedges. Arrange the slices on a large serving plate, slightly overlapping each other.

Put the tomato wedges in a bowl and drizzle with most of the olive oil and balsamic vinegar. Season to taste with salt and pepper. Mix carefully and arrange on top of the tomato slices.

Add the basil leaves and mozzarella balls to the tomato wedges. Drizzle the salad with more olive oil and balsamic vinegar, season to taste with salt and pepper, and serve.

AWARENESS POINTS

• Make it your mission to choose as many different tomatoes as possible—homegrown or store bought, you can create a full spectrum of red colors.
• Notice the way the balsamic sinks in to the intricate tears in the mozzarella. Imagine how it will add to the flavor.
• Think about presentation. Notice how the layering of ingredients adds to the impression of the dish.

Sound

Food comes with its own sounds. Think of those we make when we are eating—we chomp, crunch, grind, gulp, gnaw, munch, slurp, sputter, choke maybe, burp even. The crunchiness of potato chips, for example, has become an essential part of our enjoyment of them, and our perception of them as fresh. We think the louder they crunch, the fresher the potato chips.

The sound of calming music can make you feel peaceful and relaxed, and encourage you to stay longer at a restaurant and order another drink, or possibly a dessert. Even if you know that, I guess you may not know that sound can modulate taste, so that food tastes sweeter or more bitter, depending on the music you are listening to. Welcome to the science of "sonic seasoning."

We might think that sound has little or no impact on our eating habits, but think twice. What about the sound of the sizzling sausage in the pan, the sound of hot water boiling for the first cup of tea, the gurgling sound of the coffee machine, the crunchy potato chips, the sound of nuts cracking, the squelchy sound of a ripe peach?

Our brain recognizes the food by remembering the sounds of food we have eaten in the past. It recognizes loudness, pitch, and type, and once it has confirmed the memory of the sound, it will begin to fire up the part of the brain that desires the item.

Explore sound *Peach & blueberry crunch*

Calories per serving 371
Serves 4
Preparation time 8 minutes
Cooking time 8–10 minutes

¼ cup ground hazelnuts
¼ cup ground almonds
2 tablespoons superfine sugar
½ cup bread crumbs
1 (13½ oz) can peaches
    in natural juice
generous ¾ cup blueberries
⅔ cup heavy cream
seeds from 1 vanilla bean
1 tablespoon confectioner's sugar,
    sifted

Gently cook the ground nuts in a large skillet with the sugar and bread crumbs, stirring constantly until golden. Remove from the heat and let cool.

Put the peaches in a food processor or blender and blend with enough of the peach juice to make a thick, smooth puree.

Set aside some of the blueberries to decorate and fold the remaining blueberries gently into the puree. Spoon into 4 glasses or individual serving dishes.

Whip the cream with the vanilla seeds and confectioners' sugar until thick but not stiff and spoon evenly over the peach puree. When the crunchy topping is cool, sprinkle it over the blueberry mixture, top with the remaining blueberries, and serve.

AWARENESS POINTS

- Apply the raisin experience (see page 18) to an almond. When you slowly eat the almond, where can you hear the crunch, in what parts of your head and ears?
- What noise do the ground nuts make in the skillet. Do they hiss or rustle when the pan is shaken?
- How does the creaminess of the blueberry mixture effect the sound of the nuts when you eat them?

Touch

Touch is integral to our experience with food. It informs us about texture, moisture, chewiness, greasiness, whether the food is likely to be painful (hot chile), or astringent. By touching we know if a peach is ripe or not, we sense the smoothness of the apple, the roughness of the pear, the waxed surface of the lemon/orange, we feel if the food is heavy or light, hot or cold, wet or dry. All this information is carried to the brain where it is assessed, stimulating desire or dislike, so that we know to wait for the drink to cool down, or the peach to ripen before eating it.

Touch influences our perception of taste, too. Bread that is hard, even if the taste and smell are okay, is not pleasant. We won't eat cold oatmeal; some people don't like lukewarm milk or the feeling of edible cactus.

Explore touch *Layered nutty bars*

Calories per serving 406

Cuts into 10

Preparation time 20 minutes, plus chilling

Cooking time 5 minutes

3½ tablespoons butter

1¾ cups fat-free sweetened condensed milk

7 oz semisweet chocolate, broken into pieces

4 oz chessman cookies

⅓ cup hazelnuts

⅔ cup pistachios, shelled

Use a little of the butter to grease the bottom and sides of an 8 inch round springform pan. Put the rest of the butter in a saucepan with the condensed milk and chocolate. Heat gently for 3–4 minutes, stirring until melted, then remove from the heat.

Place the cookies in a plastic bag and crush roughly into chunky pieces using a rolling pin. Toast the hazelnuts under a preheated hot broiler until lightly browned, then coarsely chop with the pistachios.

Stir the cookies into the chocolate mixture, then spoon half the mixture into the prepared pan and spread level. Set aside 2 tablespoons of the nuts for the top, then sprinkle the rest over the chocolate cookie layer. Cover with the remaining chocolate mixture, level the surface with the back of the spoon, and sprinkle with the reserved nuts.

Chill the nut mixture for 3–4 hours until firm, then loosen the edges and remove the sides of the pan. Cut into 10 thin slices, or into tiny bite-size pieces to make petits fours. Store any leftovers in the refrigerator, wrapped in foil, for up to 3 days.

AWARENESS POINTS
- This baking recipe is great for getting your hands messy and really connecting with the food.
- Use your hands to grease the pan, noticing the coolness of the metal.
- As you add each layer of nuts and cookies to the tray, carefully push into place with your fingers, exploring and comparing the rough textures.

Taste

Flavor is important to us and what we call taste is the interconnected experience of several senses, especially smell and touch, into one single experience. When we put food into our mouth, the taste receptors on the tongue and the roof of the mouth (the taste buds) send an impulse to the brain through the cranial nerve. The brain then compares the information with stored memory of previous tastes and recognizes what you are eating. After that, it will decide if you like the taste of the food or drink, and if it is a good idea to continue consuming it.

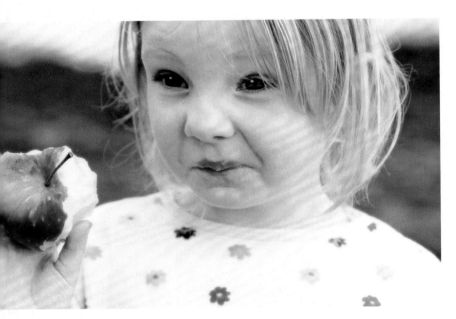

We used to refer to four tastes—sweet, bitter, sour, and salty—but recently another one, umami, has been recognized. This is found in fermented and aged foods, such as cheese and tamari (a gluten-free variety of soy sauce from Japan), and is savory.

It was once thought that these tastes were centered on different areas of the tongue but this is now no longer considered to be true. Each taste bud, no matter where it sits on the tongue, has the potential to pick up any of the five known tastes.

Explore taste *Fennel & orange casserole*

Calories per serving 232
  (not including polenta)
Serves 4
Preparation time 15 minutes
Cooking time about 50 minutes

2 fennel bulbs, trimmed
4 tablespoons extra-virgin olive oil
1 onion, chopped
2 garlic cloves, crushed
2 teaspoons chopped rosemary
scant ½ cup Pernod
1 (13 oz) can chopped tomatoes
¼ teaspoon saffron threads
2 strips of orange peel
2 tablespoons chopped fennel fronds
salt and pepper

Cut the fennel lengthwise into ¼ inch thick slices. Heat half the oil in an ovenproof casserole, add the fennel slices, in batches, and cook over medium heat for 3–4 minutes on each side until golden. Remove with a slotted spoon.

Heat the remaining oil in the casserole, add the onion, garlic, rosemary, and salt and pepper and cook over low heat, stirring frequently, for 5 minutes. Add the Pernod, bring to a boil, and boil until reduced by half. Add the tomatoes, saffron, and orange peel and stir well. Arrange the fennel slices over the top.

Bring to a boil, then cover the casserole with a tight-fitting lid and bake in a preheated oven, 350°F, for 35 minutes until the fennel is tender. Stir in the fennel fronds and serve the casserole hot with chargrilled polenta triangles, if desired.

AWARENESS POINTS

- Compare the taste of the fennel before and after cooking in stage one.
- Taste the sauce five times, focusing on, in turn, the garlic, rosemary, salt, Pernod, and orange.
- Does saffron have a taste? How would you describe it?

Breath: past, future & eating in the "now"

To learn to be with the present is not for the fainthearted. It takes courage, because it can be painful and frightening when, for example, we have just stuffed down another bout of food. To learn to be present with kind attention, we use the breath. It is always with us, easy to track, and accessible, and absolutely free. As the breath occurs only in the now, using it is an excellent way to stay present and to remind us to connect with our reality.

It is true for most of us that, for a big part of our lives, we have lived more in the past or in the future than in the present moment. Unfortunately, thinking of the past or the future will make us more stressed and agitated since we can't do anything about either of them in this moment. Hence we tend to look for something to soothe us, often food or drink.

It can be helpful to reflect on past events, so we can gain insight into what we did and why we did it, in case we need to do things differently now. Thinking about doing it differently is happening in the present moment. However, by the time we are doing it differently, it is already taking place in a new present moment (which was the future when we first thought about it). We often tend to be trapped in repetitive, negative, or attached thinking about the past and future. This can trigger a low mood, remembering all the highlights and good times we had (attachment), which alas have gone now and may never return; or it can fill us with regret (another type of low mood) about what we have done wrong or missed doing.

The future is also important, because our aspirations and intentions give us direction. Only when we know what we aspire to can we collect our energies and move toward our goal. But even if we know our goal, the first step and all those that follow happen in the present moment.

We can dream, hope, and have wonderful fantasies, but we still have to take one step at a time, and each step is occurring in the present moment. Thinking about the future can also trigger low mood, as we might compare the much more colorful and successful future of what "might be" with the reality of what actually is. Reality often lacks the splendor of our imagination.

Wherever you are at this moment, that's where you are. That is your starting point. The past is gone and the future is not yet here. It is only in this moment that we can make new and healthier choices. It is in this moment that we can start again and decide the direction of our eating life.

Experimenting with the breath

(This is largely based on breath awareness as taught by Thanissaro Bhikku.)

Sit down comfortably and keep warm.
Where do you feel the breath right now?

Is it shallow or deep, long or short, fast or slow? Has it got a rhythm? What kind of rhythm would make you feel really good?

How can you receive the breath in your body, in the lungs, and the belly, that is pleasant, enjoyable, and soothing?

See what works for you.

Try to think of the breath flowing through the entire body like waves of energy—in through the toes and up to the head, touching along its way all the nerves, blood vessels, bones.

While you are feeling the breath flowing like this, are there areas in the body where it feels blocked? What helps to unblock these areas? Breathing through them, around them, or straight into them? See what works for you. Play with the breath and discover the impact of the breath on your mind.

Notice that you are aware of your breath and you are aware of the effect it has on your well-being.

When you have found the breath pattern that gives you a sense of fullness and ease, be aware that your mind is now centered and calm.

Notice that you are aware of your breath and calm mind and now turn to awareness itself.

The more often you try this, the more often you will be able to access a calm and centered mind in your life, and also during shopping and eating.

TIPS

Bigger portions make us eat more—up to 30 percent. So be clever. Use smaller plates and smaller glasses and increase the volume of your food through extra air and water. Air and water are the cheapest ingredients to bulk up your food without adding a calorie to it. In a research project, one group of people ate fresh fruit and another group drank smoothies made with the same amount of fruit. Those who drank the smoothie felt fuller because it had been stirred for a short while and contained more volume through the air that had been whisked into it.

Don't finish all the food on your plate. For generations brought up during and after the war, this is anathema. Their parents, quite rightly, cherished food. But in some cultures, hosts stop offering you more food only when you leave some on the plate, signaling that you are full. Practice not clearing your plate and it will help you to develop the self-control you need to stop overeating, and help you to eat less.

Guided practice

Smoothies are a great way to consume food mindfully. They rely on nutritious ingredients, such as fruit and milk or yogurt with live active cultures, which nourish our bodies and provide healthy energy. They can include honey for sweetness, or avocado for savory creaminess, and it's easy to vary the recipe to omit dairy products if you prefer. Whisked to provide an airy lightness, smoothies can be sipped and savored, and are filling without being heavy.

1 We breathe deeply when we smell something pleasant. As you begin to make this smoothie, savor the delicious aroma of the sweet berries as you prepare them. Enjoy the heady scent of ripe peaches as you cut into them and release their juice. How does the skin feel to touch? When you chop fruit, or use a noisy blender to mix the ingredients, or crush ice, do you hold your breath?

2 Notice your breathing, and try to keep it slow and mindful. Appreciate the anticipation of the exotic flavor combinations, and choose a suitable glass to display the bright color of this energy-providing power drink.

3 How will you drink it? Will you sip it through a straw? Perhaps you could sit outside and enjoy the fresh air, if the weather is good enough.

4 It can be hard to drink mindfully, especially when you are thirsty. Being dehydrated can lead to consuming your meals much too fast, which in turn leads to overindulgence. Drink a large glass of water before you begin, to rehydrate your body and allow yourself to tune in to what your body requires.

5 Remember to savor the smell of the fruit as you begin to drink the smoothie. Notice the creaminess, the sharp tang of the fruit, the sweetness and the pleasant chill from the ice. Were you too hot when you started drinking it? Can you feel the cool sensation traveling through your chest, refreshing your body? Pause, and breathe deeply and mindfully between each mouthful.

6 Although blended, a smoothie is still nourishing, satisfying food, and it is important to notice when your stomach is full. When you have finished, return to the breath, and to stillness.

Fruity summer smoothie

Calories per serving 103
Makes 4 x 10 oz (1¼ cup) glasses
Preparation time 2 minutes

2 peaches, halved, pitted, and chopped
2 cups strawberries, hulled
2½ cups raspberries
1¾ cups skim or
    lowfat milk
ice cubes

Put the peaches in a blender or food processor with the strawberries and raspberries and blend to a smooth puree, scraping the mixture down from the sides of the bowl if necessary.

Add the milk and blend the ingredients again until the mixture is smooth and frothy. Pour the milkshake over the ice cubes in 4 tall glasses.

Breakfast

The intelligent body

Lost in autopilot

It seems that we have lost the ability to feel the signals the body is sending us to indicate that it is full. The body does not require calorie tables, because it knows perfectly well when to stop.

Paying attention to bodily sensations is a central part of mindful eating. As we increase our awareness, we learn to read the signs and to stop when we are full. Being in your body means you are in the present moment. It is in the now that you can feel your hunger. Unfortunately, people often eat for the future. Some people say they were eating even when they were not hungry, just to make sure they would not be hungry later in the day. By getting in touch with the body, you will relearn how it feels when you are hungry and when you are full.

The loss of innocence

Our relationship with our bodies has become complicated. We are judgmental, especially regarding image and shape—the body is ugly, disgusting, loathsome, yuk, frumpy, a blob, sordid, weak. We listen to other people talking and as we feel rejected, so we reject ourselves. By talking to ourselves like this, we miss hearing or sensing the body's subtle voice. Relearning to take notice of a light pressure in the stomach or some slight difficulty breathing as we get fuller is one of the most important goals in rebalancing our weight. Occasionally, the body's voice gets louder, or even screams. We may be feeling sick, overfull, uncomfortable. We have problems with digestion, develop heartburn. Unfortunately, most of us, most of the time, are not truly present in our bodies.

It wasn't always like this. In our childhood we didn't worry about our basic needs or how to fulfill them. The body and its innate intelligence took care of it. We slept when we were tired, and we cried when we needed food or cuddles. Our body was tirelessly and reliably working for us and supporting us as it was turning food into blood, bones, and tissue. That is what we call the intelligence of the original body.

You may wonder what causes the loss of this simple and straightforward relationship with our body that was once a natural part of life. The answer is simple and yet hard to believe. The loss occurs through the process of growing up and being taught about "civilized" behavior, including how we should walk, sit, conduct ourselves, and dress according to our gender, age, class, and culture. Mindfulness aims to bring the body and its sensations back into the field of our awareness so that once again we can feel its natural ability to pulse and flow with life.

Guided practice

1 Start the day as you mean to go on and be as kind to your body as possible. Oats are a good source of slow-release carbohydrates, and oatmeal is something we associate with comfort, warmth, and sharing. You can vary the first recipe here by adding seeds, different fruits, honeys, and syrups—it is a great dish to leave you feeling full and satisfied.

2 Everyone has their own personal preference when it comes to oatmeal consistency so enjoy the sensation of stirring the milk and watching the oats thicken. Choose your favorite bowl and spoon—perhaps someone gave them to you as a gift, they have strong memories attached, or you like the shape and color.

3 When you sit down to eat, take a moment to assess how your body feels. Register any feelings of tension. Pay attention in turn to your mouth, throat, chest, and stomach. Are you too hot or cold? Do you need to open the window or put on a sweater before you start eating? Is your stomach rumbling? Is the smell of delicious oatmeal making your mouth water? Have you had a glass of water—perhaps you are dehydrated?

4 Sit up straight, pick up the spoon carefully, and bring one small spoonful to your mouth. Test how hot it is. As you eat the first mouthful, concentrate on the sensation of the oatmeal in your mouth. Is it creamy? Is it coarse? Is the consistency just how you like it? Notice how it warms your throat, down through your chest, and into your stomach.

5 Recent studies say it takes twenty minutes before we register the feeling of fullness, so take as long to finish as possible. Savor every spoonful. See how the feeling of hunger changes and lessens. Perhaps you don't need to eat the whole bowl of oatmeal? It is all right not to finish your meal; next time you'll know to make a smaller portion. You could try pausing and putting down your spoon between mouthfuls.

6 Finally, compare how you feel now with when you started your breakfast. Do you feel full and satisfied? Is your body less tense? Enjoy the feeling of being full, but not too full—just right.

Oatmeal & prune compote

Calories per serving 259
Serves 8
Preparation time 5 minutes
Cooking time about 20 minutes

4 cups skim or lowfat milk
1 teaspoon vanilla extract
pinch of ground cinnamon
pinch of salt
2⅓ cups rolled oats
3 tablespoons slivered almonds, toasted

Compote
8 oz ready-to-eat dried Agen prunes
½ cup apple juice
1 small cinnamon stick
1 clove
1 tablespoon honey
1 unpeeled orange quarter

Place all the compote ingredients in a small saucepan over medium heat. Simmer gently for 10–12 minutes or until softened and slightly sticky. Let cool. (The compote can be prepared in advance and chilled.)

Put the milk, 2 cups water, vanilla extract, cinnamon, and salt in a large saucepan over medium heat and bring slowly to a boil. Stir in the oats, then reduce the heat and simmer gently, stirring occasionally, for 8–10 minutes until creamy and tender. Spoon the oatmeal into warmed bowls, sprinkle with the almonds, and serve with the prune compote.

Asparagus with smoked salmon

Calories per serving 150
Serves 6
Preparation time 10 minutes
Cooking time 6 minutes

7 oz trimmed asparagus

3 tablespoons coarsely chopped hazelnuts

4 teaspoons olive oil

juice of 1 lime

1 teaspoon Dijon mustard

12 quail eggs

8 oz smoked salmon

salt and pepper

AWARENESS POINTS

- Notice the fresh green of the asparagus and how it brightens as it steams
- Take your time arranging the food on the plate, and be creative—enjoy yourself!
- Mark the rich flavor of the quail eggs, the salty bite of the salmon, and the tang of the lime.

Steam the asparagus spears over a saucepan of boiling water for 5 minutes until just tender.

Meanwhile, broil the nuts on a piece of foil until lightly browned. Lightly mix together the oil, lime juice, and mustard with a little salt and pepper, then stir in the hot nuts. Keep warm.

Pour water into a saucepan to a depth of 1½ inches and bring it to a boil. Lower the eggs into the water with a slotted spoon and cook for 1 minute. Take the pan off the heat and let the eggs stand for 1 minute. Drain the eggs, rinse with cold water, and drain again.

Tear the salmon into strips and divide it among 6 serving plates, folding and twisting the strips attractively. Tuck the just-cooked asparagus into the salmon, halve the quail eggs, leaving the shells on if desired, and arrange on top. Drizzle with the warm nut dressing and serve sprinkled with a little black pepper.

Banana & golden raisin drop scones

Calories per serving 110
Makes 10
Preparation time 10 minutes
Cooking time 8 minutes

1 cup all-purpose flour
1 teaspoon baking powder
2 tablespoons superfine sugar
½ teaspoon baking powder
1 small ripe banana, about
   4 oz with skin on,
   peeled and coarsely mashed
1 egg, beaten
⅔ cup milk
¼ cup golden raisins
oil, for greasing
butter, honey, or light corn
   or maple syrup, to serve

Put the flour, baking powder, sugar, and baking powder in a mixing bowl. Add the mashed banana with the egg. Gradually whisk in the milk with a fork until the mixture resembles a smooth, thick batter. Stir in the golden raisins.

Pour a little oil onto a piece of folded paper towel and use to grease a ridged grill pan or heavy nonstick skillet. Heat the pan, then drop heaping dessertspoonfuls of the mixture, well spaced apart, onto the pan. Cook for 2 minutes until bubbles appear on the top and the undersides are golden. Turn over and cook for another 1–2 minutes until cooked.

Serve warm, each topped with 1 teaspoon butter, honey, light corn, or maple syrup. These are best eaten on the day they are made.

AWARENESS POINTS

- Notice the sweet smell of the ripe banana before you make the scones.
- Mark the changing texture as you whisk the batter—is there a point at which it begins to require more effort?
- Taste the topping options, one at a time, with your eyes closed, and decide which you prefer.

Guided practice

A cooked breakfast tends to signify an occasion. Eggs play a huge part in any celebratory breakfast or brunch and are a great protein-rich way to start the day. Take the time to appreciate where the eggs have come from. Have you checked they are reliably sourced? More and more people are keeping chickens and growing their own food stuff so perhaps these eggs come from even closer to home.

1 Notice the way the smells in the kitchen change as you add the ingredients to the hot pan. How does it affect your appetite? How long before the onion and garlic start to sizzle? Ras El Hanout is extremely distinctive—does it evoke any memories of travels or other Moroccan dishes you may have tried? What do you notice about the texture of the coriander and how does it change when it begins to cook?

2 How you like the consistency of your eggs is a personal choice so make sure you have taken the time to work out your preference. Try to make this a breakfast that is exactly to your taste, and for no one else. If you are eating with someone else, serve the individual pots different ways if needs be.

3 Make every bite count. See if you can distinguish the sharpness of the cherry tomatoes against the garlic and ras el hanout. How would you describe the taste of the yolk compared to the cooked egg white? With the next bite see if you can you make out the very subtle pinch of cinnamon.

Moroccan baked eggs

Calories per serving 170
Serves 2
Preparation time 10 minutes
Cooking time 25–35 minutes

½ tablespoon olive oil
½ onion, chopped
1 garlic clove, sliced
½ teaspoon ras el hanout
pinch ground cinnamon
½ teaspoon ground coriander
13 oz cherry tomatoes
2 tablespoons chopped cilantro leaves
2 eggs
salt and pepper

Heat the oil in a skillet over medium heat, add the onion and garlic, and cook for 6–7 minutes or until softened and lightly golden, stirring occasionally. Stir in the spices and cook for another 1 minute. Add the tomatoes and season well with salt and pepper, then simmer gently for 8–10 minutes. Sprinkle over 3 teaspoons of the cilantro, then divide the tomato mixture between 2 individual ovenproof dishes. Break an egg into each dish.

Bake in a preheated oven, 425°F, for 8–10 minutes until the egg is set but the yolks are still slightly runny. Cook for another 2–3 minutes if you prefer the eggs to be cooked through. Serve sprinkled with the remaining cilantro.

Figs with yogurt & honey

Calories per serving 105
Serves 4
Preparation time 5 minutes
Cooking time 10 minutes

8 ripe figs
4 tablespoons plain yogurt
2 tablespoons honey

Slice the figs in half and place on a hot ridged grill pan, skin side down. Sear for 10 minutes until the skins begin to blacken, then remove.

Arrange the figs on 4 plates and serve with a spoonful of yogurt and the honey spooned over the top.

For brioche French toasts with figs, yogurt & honey, brush 4 slices of brioche with a mixture of 3½ tablespoons melted butter and scant ¼ cup light cream and toast under a preheated broiler. Top with figs, as above.

AWARENESS POINTS
- Notice the beautiful natural shape of the split figs.
- Take a slow mouthful of fig, honey, and yogurt. Enjoy the contrast of the fibrous fruit with the sticky sweet honey and the sharp, sour yogurt.
- Think about the energy and the nutrition you will gain from eating this healthy, luxurious breakfast.

Nutty passion fruit yogurts

Calories per serving 348

Serves 2

Preparation time 5 minutes, plus chilling

2 passion fruit

1 cup plain yogurt

4 tablespoons honey

⅓ cup hazelnuts, toasted and coarsely chopped

4 clementines, peeled and chopped into small pieces

AWARENESS POINTS

- Touch the various textures of the passion fruit: the pulpy center, the seeds, the hard skin.
- For visual impact, make sure all the ingredients can be seen in their various contrasting layers through the side of the glass.
- Mark the difference between the crunchy and the soft texture as you swallow.

Halve the passion fruit and scoop the pulp into a large bowl. Add the yogurt and mix them together gently.

Put 2 tablespoonfuls of the honey in the bases of 2 narrow glasses and sprinkle with half of the hazelnuts. Spoon half of the yogurt over the nuts and arrange half of the clementine pieces on top of the yogurt.

Repeat the layering, setting aside a few of the nuts for decoration. Sprinkle the nuts over the top and chill the yogurts until you are ready to serve them.

For passion fruit, coconut & strawberry yogurts, soak 2 tablespoons dry unsweetened coconut in 4 tablespoons skim milk for 30 minutes. Mix the passion fruit and yogurt as above, also folding in the soaked coconut. Layer as above, omitting the hazelnuts and replacing the clementines with ⅔ cup quartered strawberries.

Very berry & fromage frais fool

Calories per serving 219

Serves 4

Preparation time 5 minutes, plus cooling and chilling

Cooking time about 5 minutes

3 tablespoons crème de cassis or spiced red fruit cordial

1¾ cups mixed frozen berries

2–4 tablespoons confectioners' sugar, to taste

2 cups fat-free fromage frais

1 cup low-fat black currant yogurt

1 vanilla bean, split in half lengthwise

toasted slivered almonds, to serve

Put the crème de cassis or cordial in a saucepan over low heat and gently heat, then add the berries. Stir, cover, and cook for about 5 minutes or until the fruit has thawed and is beginning to collapse. Remove from the heat and stir in 1–3 tablespoons of the confectioners' sugar, according to taste. Let cool completely, then chill for at least 1 hour.

Mix together the fromage frais, yogurt, and 1 tablespoon of the confectioners' sugar in a bowl. Scrape in the seeds from the vanilla bean and beat to combine. Fold the berries into the fromage frais mixture until just combined. Carefully spoon into 4 decorative glasses or glass serving dishes and serve immediately, sprinkled with toasted almonds, if desired.

AWARENESS POINTS

- Taste the berries as you add the sugar, stopping at the point where they are just sweet enough.
- Enjoy the creamy, comforting smell of vanilla as you scrape the bean and stir the fool mixture.
- Think about who you will share this with. Offer them a choice of toppings, such as muesli or nuts.

Apricot tea bread

Calories per serving 230

Cuts into 10

Preparation time 25 minutes, plus soaking

Cooking time 1 hour

½ cup ready-to-eat dried apricots, chopped

½ cup golden raisins

⅔ cup raisins

¾ cup superfine sugar

butter, for greasing and to serve

1¼ cups hot strong tea

2¼ cups all-purpose flour

2 teaspoons baking powder

1 teaspoon baking soda

1 teaspoon ground cinnamon

1 egg, beaten

AWARENESS POINTS

- Share this wholesome gift with friends and family to show them your gratitude for the small things they do for you.
- As you add the hot tea, take a moment to inhale the sweet, exotically scented steam.
- Try the bread with salted and unsalted butter, marking the contrast.

Put the dried fruits and sugar in a mixing bowl, add the hot tea, and mix together. Let soak for 4 hours or overnight.

Grease a 2 lb loaf pan and line its bottom and 2 long sides with greased nonstick parchment paper. Mix the flour, baking powder, baking soda, and cinnamon together, add to the soaked fruit with the beaten egg, and mix together well.

Spoon into the prepared pan and spread the surface level, then bake in the center of a preheated oven, 325°F, for about 1 hour until well risen, the top has cracked, and a skewer inserted into the center comes out clean.

Let cool in the pan for 10 minutes, then loosen the edges and lift out of the pan using the lining paper. Transfer to a wire rack, peel off the lining paper, and let cool completely. Cut into 10 slices and spread with a little butter to serve. This tea bread can be stored, unbuttered, in an airtight tin for up to 1 week.

Granola squares

Calories per serving 399

Makes 12

Preparation time 15 minutes, plus chilling

Cooking time 20 minutes

1½ sticks (12 tablespoons) butter, plus extra for greasing

⅔ cup honey

2 tablespoons maple syrup

1 teaspoon ground cinnamon

¾ cup ready-to-eat dried apricots, coarsely chopped

3½ oz ready-to-eat dried papaya or mango, coarsely chopped

¾ cup raisins

4 tablespoons pumpkin seeds

2 tablespoons sesame seeds

3 tablespoons sunflower seeds

½ cup pecans, coarsely chopped

3¼ cups rolled oats

Grease a 11 x 7 inch deep jelly roll pan with butter and line the bottom with nonstick parchment paper.

Place the butter, honey, and maple syrup in a medium saucepan and heat, stirring continually, until the butter has melted. Add the cinnamon, dried fruit, seeds, and nuts, stir the mixture, and heat for 1 minute. Remove from the heat and add the rolled oats, stirring until they are well coated in the syrup.

Transfer the mixture to the prepared pan and smooth down with the back of a spoon to compact into the pan and level. Bake in a preheated oven, 350°F, for 15 minutes until the top is just beginning to brown. Let cool in the pan, then chill in the refrigerator for 30–60 minutes.

Turn out the chilled granola, upside down, on a cutting board, then carefully flip it back over to its correct side. Using a long, sharp knife (preferably longer than the granola itself), cut into 12 squares.

AWARENESS POINTS

- Taste the dried ingredients— are they sweet, chewy, hard, or bitter?
- Enjoy the aroma of butter, honey, and syrup warming in the pan as it suffuses your kitchen.
- See whether you can taste the individual nuts and seeds in the granola—is the sesame there, and can you detect the cinnamon?

Mango & vanilla muffin slice

Calories per serving 336

Cuts into 8

Preparation time 20 minutes

Cooking time 1 hour

7 tablespoons slightly salted butter, melted, plus extra for greasing

1 small ripe mango

1¾ cups all-purpose flour

2 teaspoons baking powder

¾ cup superfine sugar

½ cup rolled oats

1 egg, beaten

¾ cup milk

1 teaspoon vanilla bean paste or extract

vanilla sugar, for sprinkling

AWARENESS POINTS

- Enjoy the methodical, careful process of cutting a mango.
- Notice the homely smell of baking and how it differs with the addition of exotic mango.
- Serve with your favorite tea, brewed just to your liking.

Grease a 2 lb loaf pan with butter and line with nonstick parchment paper.

Halve the mango each side of the flat central seed. Cut away the seed, then peel and dice the flesh into ¼ inch pieces.

Sift the flour and baking powder into a bowl, then stir in the superfine sugar and oats. Beat together the egg, milk, vanilla, and melted butter in a small bowl. Add to the dry ingredients with half the mango and stir together using a large metal spoon until just combined.

Spoon the batter into the prepared pan and sprinkle with the remaining mango pieces. Bake in a preheated oven, 350°F, for about 1 hour or until well risen, firm to the touch, and a skewer inserted into the center comes out clean.

Let cool in the pan for 5 minutes, then loosen at the ends and transfer to a wire rack to cool. Peel off the lining paper and serve warm or cold, sprinkled with vanilla sugar.

Lunch

Moving with a mindful mind

Mindful movement can be a way of getting you off the couch, so that you can start enjoying simple activities such as walking again. But the "mindfulness" factor can also be an important addition to an existing workout routine.

Mindful movement

The mindful form of exercise brings you back in touch with your body through movement. The founding father of mindfulness within the secular world, Jon Kabat-Zinn, introduced yoga into his program because he had found it to be enjoyable in his own life. As he said in 1990, "The focus is on maintaining moment-to-moment awareness of the sensations accompanying our movements, letting go of any thoughts or feelings about the sensations themselves."

Mindfulness flourishes under what are called the seven attitudinal foundations of mindfulness. Knowing them will help you to differentiate between a normal practice and a mindful movement practice.

The seven attitudinal foundations are:
  Nonjudging
  Patience
  Beginner's mind (childlike curiosity)
  Trust
  Nonstriving
  Acceptance
  Letting go

If your exercise teacher (and remember you are your own teacher when you practice at home) enables you to integrate these elements into your movement practice, you are on the right track.

In fact any activity done with a mindful attitude can help you to get through the day with ease, calm, and enough energy to keep going. On top of that you can discover gifts of tranquillity and focus you thought you could never have. Encourage yourself to engage in a movement practice you really like (how about dancing!?) and it can help you to relieve the stress that has been stored in your body. Mindful movement can bring you a feeling of coming home, to the here and now, through self-acceptance, awareness, and kindness.

A short yoga practice

Free up the neck: sit on a chair, looking ahead, then allow the chin to drop onto the breastbone. Then look up again. Repeat a few times and be very mindful of the movement that occurs in your neck/cervical spine. Come back to the start position and feel the neck now.

Sit upright, look ahead, and let the head drop forward onto the chest. Now gently let the head sway left and right in small movements like a pendulum. Follow the movement attentively. When you have repeated it 5–7 times come back to the upright position and feel the neck now.

Free up the shoulders: you can do this movement sitting, lying down, or even in the morning before you get out of bed. With the arms along the sides of the body, draw the right shoulder up toward the ear and let it sink back to the start position. Repeat several times, then stop and sense into the upper body and shoulder. Then draw the right shoulder forward and back. Repeat several times and come back to the start position. Feel the upper body and shoulder now. Then bring these two movements together and start to circle the right shoulder. When you have finished, compare the right side with the left. Do you notice any difference? In size, temperature, weight, length? Now repeat on the other side and then circle both shoulders together.

Mindful walking

Most of us can engage in a practical exercise such as walking. It is safe, doesn't cost anything, and with proper clothing can be done anytime and anywhere. It can be done whether you are old or young, stiff or mobile, healthy and fit, or recovering from illness and exhaustion. Walking can accommodate each one of us, whoever we are, whatever condition we are in. It has many health benefits, as it conditions the heart and lungs, burns calories, and helps to destress by expelling stale air from the lungs. The goal is not to reach any destination but to develop understanding and awareness of the sensations that occur in the body while you are walking.

Become aware of the muscles and the joints in your body as you move. Start with some slow steps and notice how your foot makes contact with the ground. Then pay attention to the lifting of the heel and the push-off from the toes, the weight distribution on your foot, the engagement of your calf muscles and hamstrings, and the ankle, knee, and hip joints. Notice your trunk swaying and your arms swinging. Start to playfully increase your speed, but remember, it is not about reaching any destination: your goal is awareness of the body moving.

Scan your body from head to toes for any unnecessary tension. Be aware of the areas around the neck, shoulders, and lower back. Ask yourself what is needed to make this movement light and enjoyable. Lengthen your stride and as you do so see if your arms can swing a bit further. Try to lead the movement from your pelvis and navel center, rather than from your head or chest. Walk for at least 10 minutes and then gradually reduce your pace.

Guided practice

1 After any activity, your energy levels need restoring. Energy comes from carbohydrates and while some of these should be eaten in moderation, plenty of others are extremely healthy and can be eaten as part of a mindful diet. Protein is also essential for healthy, strong muscles, and it helps you to feel full for longer.

2 The recipes in this section have been chosen to provide you with the right sort of energy and balanced nutrition for an active lifestyle. It is important to balance movement with rest. Your lung capacity improves with exercise. The freeness of breath, exhilaration, and release of endorphins produce a fantastic rush, but it is important to take the time to enjoy this as well as to contrast the experience with calm and stillness. Return to slow breathing and find the stillness and peace required for mindful eating.

3 This first recipe here is quick, easy, and versatile —excellent for those with a busy, active lifestyle. Salmon is great source of protein and essential oils. Its vibrant color is always a delight to look at and as the bright red warms to a delicate pink, you can appreciate every stage of the cooking process. Bulgur wheat is rich in protein and minerals and has a nutty taste. It provides an excellent contrast to the flaky, oily salmon and crisp green vegetables.

4 As you eat, notice how your body receives the food. Let it reward your movement and restore your energy levels. Remember to eat slowly, returning the body and breath to a state of stillness and peace. It is common for people who have exercised to overeat and treat food as a reward, so remember to pause frequently and really listen to your body's fullness signals.

5 In particular, the zingy lemon will bring out the light flavor of the salmon. Appreciate how fresh that feels with the green vegetables. Imagine every mouthful is helping to restore your body. Take time to appreciate how energized and satisfied you feel.

Salmon & bulgur wheat pilaf

Calories per serving 478
Serves 4
Preparation time 10 minutes
Cooking time 10–15 minutes

15 oz boneless, skinless salmon
1½ cups bulgur wheat
¾ cup frozen peas
7 oz string beans, chopped
2 tablespoons chopped chives
2 tablespoons chopped flat-leaf parsley
salt and pepper

To serve
2 lemons, halved
low-fat yogurt

Cook the salmon in a steamer or microwave for about 10 minutes. Alternatively, wrap it in aluminum foil and cook in a preheated oven, 350°F, for 15 minutes.

Meanwhile, cook the bulgur wheat according to the directions on the package and boil the peas and beans. Alternatively, cook the bulgur wheat, peas, and beans in the steamer with the salmon.

Flake the salmon and mix it into the bulgur wheat with the peas and beans. Fold in the chives and parsley and season to taste. Serve immediately with lemon halves and yogurt.

Cream of leek & pea soup

Calories per serving 322
Serves 4
Preparation time 15 minutes
Cooking time 25 minutes

2 tablespoons olive oil
12 oz leeks, trimmed, cleaned,
   and thinly sliced
3¾ cups fresh shelled
   or frozen peas
3½ cups vegetable stock
1 small bunch of mint
⅔ cup whole mascarpone cheese
grated zest of 1 small lemon
salt and pepper

To garnish (optional)
mint leaves
lemon zest curls

Heat the oil in a saucepan, add the leeks, and toss in the oil, then cover and fry gently for 10 minutes, stirring occasionally, until softened but not colored. Mix in the peas and cook briefly.

Pour the stock into the pan, add a little salt and pepper, then bring to a boil. Cover and simmer gently for 10 minutes. Ladle half the soup into a blender or food processor, add the mint, and blend until smooth. Pour the puree back into the saucepan.

Mix the mascarpone with half the lemon zest, reserving the rest for a garnish. Spoon half the mixture into the soup, then reheat, stirring until the mascarpone has melted. Taste and adjust the seasoning if needed. Ladle the soup into 4 warmed bowls, top with spoonfuls of the remaining mascarpone, and a sprinkling of the remaining lemon zest. Garnish with mint leaves and lemon rind curls, if desired.

AWARENESS POINTS

- Shelling peas is a repetitive task so why not sit somewhere relaxing or listen to music as you do it.
- Enjoy the vivid, bright green colors. Smell the mint leaves and lemon zest curls— appreciate the freshness and note down any emotions. Perhaps it makes you think of the outdoors.
- Serve in your favorite bowl, taking the time to garnish the soup so it looks impressive and reflects your efforts.

Fruity stuffed peppers

Calories per serving 421

Serves 4

Preparation time 15 minutes

Cooking time 1 hour

2 red bell peppers, cored, seeded, and halved

2 orange bell peppers, cored, seeded, and halved

2 tablespoons olive oil, plus extra for brushing

1 red onion, chopped

1 garlic clove, crushed

1 small red chile, seeded and finely chopped

¼ cup pine nuts

generous 1⅛ cups cooked wild rice

1 (13 oz) can green lentils, rinsed and drained

8 oz cherry tomatoes, quartered

½ cup ready-to-eat dried apricots, chopped

handful of golden raisins

grated zest of 1 lemon

2 tablespoons chopped fresh herbs

⅔ cup crumbled feta cheese

AWARENESS POINTS

- Notice the fresh, bittersweet smell as you prepare the peppers.
- Take a small mouthful and chew slowly, noticing the different tastes and textures.
- Which is your favorite combination?

Put the peppers in an ovenproof dish, cut side up, and brush each with a little oil. Place in a preheated oven, 400°F, for 20 minutes.

Meanwhile, heat the oil in skillet, add the onion, garlic, and chile and fry for 2 minutes, then add the pine nuts and cook for another 2 minutes until golden. Stir in all the remaining ingredients.

Remove the peppers from the oven and spoon the stuffing mixture into the peppers. Cover with aluminum foil, return to the oven, and cook for 25 minutes, then remove the foil and cook for another 15 minutes. Serve with a crisp salad.

Hot & sour soup

Calories per serving 161
Serves 4
Preparation time 10 minutes
Cooking time 12 minutes

3 cups vegetable or fish stock

4 dried kaffir lime leaves

1 inch piece of fresh ginger root, peeled
  and grated

1 red chile, seeded and sliced

1 lemon grass stalk, lightly bruised

1¾ cups sliced mushrooms

3½ oz rice noodles

3 oz baby spinach leaves

4 oz cooked, peeled tiger shrimp, or
  defrosted if frozen, rinsed with cold
  water, and drained

2 tablespoons lemon juice

black pepper

AWARENESS POINTS

- Feel the different hard and soft
  textures you are preparing.
- Consider the smell of lemon
  grass. Does it seem savory
  or sweet?
- Note the riot of colors and
  shapes in this dish.

Put the stock, lime leaves, fresh ginger root, chile, and
lemon grass in a large saucepan. Cover and bring to a
boil. Add the mushrooms and simmer for 2 minutes.
Break the noodles into short lengths, drop into the soup,
and simmer for 3 minutes.

Add the baby spinach and shrimp and simmer for
2 minutes until the shrimp are heated through. Add the
lemon juice. Remove and discard the lemon grass stalk
and season the soup with black pepper before serving.

Arugula, pear & pecorino salad

Calories per serving 195
Serves 4
Preparation time 10 minutes

8 oz arugula leaves
2 pears, quartered and cored
3 oz pecorino cheese shavings

Dressing
1 teaspoon Dijon mustard
2 tablespoons cider vinegar
2 tablespoons olive oil
salt and pepper

AWARENESS POINTS
- Notice the peppery taste of the arugula.
- How does it change the flavor of the pears?
- Think about what size fruit slices will work best for flavor and presentation.

Make the dressing. Whisk together the mustard, cider vinegar, and oil. Season to taste with salt and pepper.

Put the arugula in a large salad bowl. Finely slice the pears and add them to the arugula. Add the dressing to the salad and toss carefully to mix.

Layer most of the pecorino shavings through the arugula and pear salad, garnish with the remaining shavings, and serve.

For arugula, apple & balsamic salad, combine 8 oz arugula leaves, 1 finely sliced green apple, and 3 oz pecorino cheese shavings in a large salad bowl. Whisk together 2 tablespoons aged balsamic vinegar and 3 tablespoons olive oil. Add the dressing to the salad, toss carefully to mix, and serve immediately.

Guided practice

Part of Mindful cooking is to experiment with flavors and use your intuition. Listen to your body and adapt the recipe to suit your needs. As with many of the salads in this chapter, you can apply basic nutrition and swap ingredients for your choice of protein, fruit, vegetables, nuts, and seeds.

1 Celery has a high water content. After cutting, take a bite-size amount and notice how the water explodes in your mouth as you slowly chew. What noise does it make, what is the texture? Do the same with the apricots and the almonds. Can you rate their textures from smooth to wrinkled, soft to hard, chewy to brittle?

2 Salads should never feel dull or boring so garnish this dish like it is a work of art. Make sure your plate looks full of food you are tempted to eat. Try and get all the elements of the salad onto the fork and savor all the flavors at once. Chew each mouthful 20–30 times and then put the fork down. Take a breath. Imagine you are at the height of your day, your energy levels are at their peak, your body needs to feel strong and lively.

3 Finally, make sure you take a full lunch hour and get a change of scenery. Take the time to notice how you feel after your lunch. Have you had time to digest? Have you eaten just the right amount so that you don't feel uncomfortable and lethargic?

Chicken & apricot salad

Calories per serving 366
Serves 4
Preparation time 15 minutes

7 oz celery
½ cup almonds, coarsely chopped
3 tablespoons chopped parsley
4 tablespoons mayonnaise
3 poached or roasted chicken breasts,
  each about 5 oz, shredded
12 fresh apricots, halved and pitted
salt and pepper

Thinly slice the celery stalks diagonally,
reserving the yellow inner leaves. Transfer
to a large salad bowl together with half
the leaves. Add half the almonds to the bowl
with the parsley and mayonnaise. Season
to taste with salt and pepper.

Arrange the salad on a serving plate.
Add the chicken and apricots to the salad
and stir lightly to combine.

Garnish with the remaining almonds
and celery leaves and serve.

Beet, spinach & orange salad

Calories per serving 221

Serves 4

Preparation time 20 minutes,
   plus cooling

Cooking time 1–2 hours

1 lb uncooked beets, preferably of a
   similar size

2 garlic cloves, peeled
   and left whole

handful of oregano leaves

1 teaspoon vegetable oil

1 tablespoon balsamic vinegar

7 oz baby spinach leaves

2 oranges, peeled, white pith removed,
   and cut into segments

salt and pepper

Vinaigrette

1 tablespoon balsamic vinegar

1 teaspoon Dijon mustard

4 tablespoons olive oil

pinch of sugar (optional)

Put the whole beets in the center of a large piece of aluminum foil, along with the garlic and oregano. Sprinkle with pepper and drizzle over the vegetable oil and vinegar. Gather up the foil loosely and fold over at the top to seal it. Place on a baking sheet and bake in a preheated oven, 400°F, for 1–2 hours (depending on how large the beets are) until tender. Unwrap the foil package and let the beets cool before peeling and slicing them. Discard the garlic.

Make the vinaigrette. Mix together the balsamic vinegar and mustard in a small bowl. Season with a little salt and pepper. Gradually add the olive oil, whisking constantly, until smooth and well combined. Taste and adjust the seasoning as needed, adding a pinch of sugar to reduce the acidity, if desired, bearing in mind the sweetness of the roasted beets. Whisk again until the sugar has dissolved. Alternatively, put all the vinaigrette ingredients in a screw-top jar, seal tightly, and shake vigorously until well combined.

Put the spinach in a large bowl, then gently toss together with the beets and oranges. Drizzle over the vinaigrette and sprinkle with pepper.

AWARENESS POINTS

- Buy local or organic beets if you can.
- Take time to appreciate the smell of roasting garlic and oregano.
- Enjoy the contrast of earthy beet with sharp vinaigrette and sweet orange.

Shrimp with black sesame seeds

Calories per serving 132
Serves 4 (with 2 other main dishes)
Preparation time 10 minutes
Cooking time about 10 minutes

½ tablespoon black sesame seeds

1½ tablespoons sunflower oil

2–3 garlic cloves, finely chopped

8 oz raw shrimp, peeled and deveined, with tails left intact

7 oz water chestnuts, drained and thinly sliced

4 oz snow peas, trimmed

2 tablespoons vegetable stock, seafood stock, or water

1 tablespoon light soy sauce

1 tablespoon oyster sauce

AWARENESS POINTS

- Be aware of the fragrance of the seeds as you cook them.
- Note the changing colors of the garlic and the shrimp.
- Mark the fresh crunchiness of the snow peas and water chestnuts.

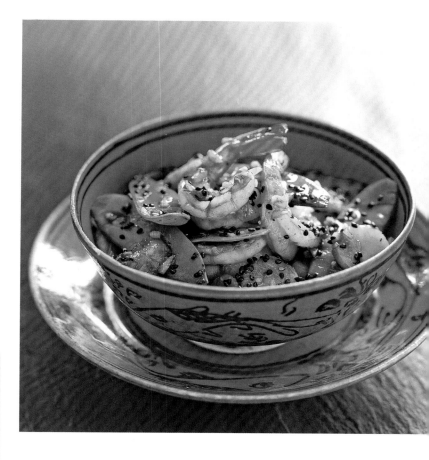

Dry-fry the black sesame seeds in a small pan for 1–2 minutes or until fragrant, then set aside.

Heat the oil in a wok or large skillet and stir-fry the garlic over medium heat until it is lightly browned.

Add the shrimp, water chestnuts, and snow peas and stir-fry over high heat for 1–2 minutes. Add the stock, soy sauce, and oyster sauce and stir-fry for another 2–3 minutes or until the shrimp open and turn pink. Stir in the fried sesame seeds and serve immediately.

Aromatic chicken pancakes

Calories per serving 269

Serves 4

Preparation time 10 minutes

Cooking time 7 minutes

4 boneless, skinless chicken breasts, about 5 oz each
6 tablespoons hoisin sauce

To serve
12 Chinese pancakes, warmed
½ cucumber, cut into matchsticks
12 scallions, thinly sliced
handful of fresh cilantro
4 tablespoons hoisin sauce mixed with 3 tablespoons water

Lay a chicken breast between 2 sheets of plastic wrap and flatten with a rolling pin or meat mallet until it is 1 inch thick. Repeat with the remaining chicken breasts. Transfer to a baking sheet and brush with some of the hoisin sauce.

Cook the chicken breasts under a preheated hot broiler for 4 minutes. Turn them over, brush with the remaining hoisin sauce, and cook for another 3 minutes or until the chicken is cooked through.

Meanwhile, warm the pancakes in a bamboo steamer for 3 minutes or until heated through.

Slice the chicken thinly and arrange it on a serving plate. Serve with the pancakes, accompanied by the cucumber, scallions, cilantro, and diluted hoisin sauce in separate bowls, so that everyone can assemble their own pancakes.

AWARENESS POINTS

- Chop the scallions and cucumber into long, thin strips to echo their natural shapes. Notice how delicate and light the matchstick vegetables feel.

- Smell and taste the hoisin sauce. Can you detect soy, chiles, or garlic? Notice how the sweet and salty sauce highlights the savory duck flavor.

- This meal is great to share and allows others to get involved. Encourage people to assemble and wrap their own pancakes. Note how people's tastes vary.

Greek country salad with halloumi

Calories per serving 398

Serves 4

Preparation time 10 minutes

Cooking time 2 minutes

4 vine-ripened tomatoes, coarsely
   chopped

½ onion, sliced

1 Lebanese cucumber,
   thickly sliced

½ cup pitted black Kalamata olives

1 small cos lettuce

8 oz halloumi cheese, sliced

Dressing

4 tablespoons extra-virgin olive oil

1½ tablespoons red wine vinegar

1 teaspoon dried oregano

salt and pepper

Put the tomatoes, onion, cucumber, and olives in a bowl. Tear the lettuce into pieces and add to the salad. Toss well and arrange on a large platter.

Whisk all the dressing ingredients together in a small bowl and season with salt and pepper. Drizzle a little over the salad.

Heat a heavy skillet until hot, add the halloumi slices, and cook for 1 minute on each side until they are charred and softened. Arrange on top of the salad, drizzle over the remaining dressing, and serve.

For Greek salad with chunky croutons, replace the halloumi with 1⅓ cups crumbled feta cheese. To make the croutons, cut thick slices of close-textured country bread, then cut these into large chunks. Heat a little olive oil in a skillet and fry the bread, turning occasionally, until crisp and golden. Add extra olive oil as needed. Cool, then toss into the salad and serve.

AWARENESS POINTS

- Do you know what types of olives you like? Take the time to sample different types.
- Enjoy the bright colors as you combine the ingredients.
- Notice how the flavors of oregano and halloumi enhance one another.

Lime & coconut squid

Calories per serving 452

Serves 2

Preparation time 15 minutes

Cooking time 5 minutes

10–12 prepared baby squid, about 12 oz including tentacles, cleaned

4 limes, halved

Dressing

2 red chiles, seeded and finely chopped

finely grated zest and juice of 2 limes

1 inch piece of fresh ginger root, peeled and grated

1½ cups freshly shredded coconut

4 tablespoons peanut oil

1–2 tablespoons chili oil

1 tablespoon white wine vinegar

Cut down the side of each squid so that they can be laid flat on a cutting board. Using a sharp knife, lightly score the inside flesh in a crisscross pattern.

Mix all the dressing ingredients together in a bowl. Toss the squid in half the dressing until thoroughly coated.

Heat a ridged grill pan until smoking hot, add the limes, cut side down, and cook for 2 minutes or until well charred. Remove from the pan and set aside. Keeping the grill pan very hot, add the squid pieces and cook for 1 minute. Turn them over and cook for another minute or until they turn white, lose their transparency, and are charred.

Transfer the squid to a cutting board and cut into strips. Drizzle with the remaining dressing and serve immediately with the charred limes and a salad of mixed salad greens.

AWARENESS POINTS

- Source your seafood with care, and buy ethically.
- As you grate the ginger, notice the spicy, sweet smell.
- Enjoy the contrast of the charred, sweet/sour limes with the spicy dressing.

Seared chicken sandwiches

Calories per serving 293

Serves 4

Preparation time 15 minutes

Cooking time 5–6 minutes

8 oz mini chicken breasts

8 teaspoons balsamic vinegar

8 slices of granary bread

6 tablespoons low-fat plain yogurt

½–1 teaspoon freshly shredded hot
    horseradish or horseradish sauce,
    to taste

3½ oz mixed salad greens with
    beet strips

pepper

AWARENESS POINTS

- Sample a tiny drop of balsamic vinegar, noticing its thick texture and sweetness.
- Mixing the yogurt with horseradish, taste frequently and notice how the heat increases.
- Layer the sandwich ingredients carefully to present their colors.

Put the mini chicken breasts into a plastic bag with half the vinegar and toss together until evenly coated.

Heat a nonstick skillet, lift the chicken out of the plastic bag with a fork, and add the pieces to the pan. Fry for 3 minutes, turn, and drizzle with the vinegar from the bag and cook for another 2–3 minutes or until browned and cooked through.

Toast the bread lightly on both sides. Slice the chicken into long, thin strips. Mix together the yogurt and horseradish and a little pepper to taste. Add the salad greens and toss together.

Arrange the yogurt and salad greens on 4 slices of toast, then add some chicken strips, drizzle over the remaining vinegar, if desired, and top with the remaining slices of toast. Cut each sandwich in half and serve immediately.

For tangy chicken, lemon & garlic toasties, toss the chicken fillets with the juice of ½ lemon and 1 tablespoon olive oil, then fry as above omitting the vinegar. Toast 8 slices of wholewheat bread, then spread with 4 tablespoons reduced-fat garlic mayonnaise. Divide the chicken between 4 slices of toast then top with the shredded leaves of 2 Boston lettuces and a 2 inch piece of cucumber, thinly sliced. Cover with the remaining slices of toast, then press together and cut into triangles.

Griddled vegetable platter

Calories per serving 285
  (not including bread)

Serves 4

Preparation time 10 minutes,
  plus marinating

Cooking time 20–30 minutes

2 zucchini, sliced lengthwise into
  ¼ inch thick slices

1 eggplant, sliced lengthwise into
  ¼ inch thick slices

1 yellow bell pepper, cored, seeded, and
  cut into 1 inch thick slices

1 red bell pepper, cored, seeded, and cut
  into 1 inch thick slices

scant ½ cup extra-virgin olive oil

2 garlic cloves, crushed

large pinch of crushed dried chiles

handful of small mint and/or basil
  leaves

salt

Toss all the prepared vegetables in 2 tablespoons of the oil until well coated.

Heat a ridged grill pan over high heat until smoking hot. Add the zucchini and eggplant in batches and cook for 2–3 minutes on each side. Transfer to a bowl and toss with the remaining oil, the garlic, and crushed dried chiles. Set aside.

Add the peppers in batches to the reheated grill pan and cook for 3–4 minutes on each side, then combine with the zucchini and eggplant. Season with salt and toss in the herbs.

Cover and let marinate at room temperature for 30 minutes. Serve with slices of country bread, if desired.

AWARENESS POINTS

- Vary the vegetables according to season and local availability.
- Enjoy the sound, smells, and heat as they sizzle.
- Arrange the vegetables creatively so that their bright colors stand out.

Making connections

Some of us feel that something is missing from our lives and we tend to try to fill this emptiness with food.

If you ask yourself what you are really longing for and what it is that brings you true happiness, what would you answer? Many people say that they want to live together in peace, free from torture and war. To live in a world where there is enough for all to share, and to protect the beauty of the planet. But when we look at the daily news another picture emerges.

In our so-called civilized society, we have to face up to leaders who seem to care more about what is best for them rather than for the whole of society, and who live with greed, dishonesty, and corruption.

We can't change them, but we can make small changes in our own lives. One way to do this is by eating together. How many families eat their meals separately? Sharing a meal with others can truly enrich your life. By cooking and eating together, even just for an evening, you can create a community that has values, such as not turning away strangers in need for food.

Conclusion

The food we eat and the food we buy matters. By being mindful, we build connections with others and make better choices. We understand what we really want. Mindfulness encourages us to enjoy the food in front of us, simple or rich, whether alone or with others, and reminds us that this is the first step. Try to go deeper and discover the inner nourishment of feeling your human connectedness and you will become less self-centered and more open. If you can achieve this, you will change your eating habits because you will know the impact you are having on others.

More ideas

It's not just baking bread that brings a happiness reward. Baking other food is a great way to spend an afternoon or weekend. From batches of scones to trays of cupcakes, you can chart the mindful journey it takes you on. Making jam is a great way to use homegrown fruit and to recycle jars (be sure to sterilize them first), and batch cooking can be great for busy professionals. Cook a hearty soup or stew that can be kept or frozen, so you can quickly heat up a healthy meal after work.

Guided practice

A perfect roast meal will bring friends and family together. When you cook this recipe, spend some time thinking about what you are really trying to achieve—is it the perfect cooking result, or meaningful time spent with loved ones? Perhaps it is a celebration, or an anniversary, or the opportunity to catch up with someone you haven't seen in a long time.

1 Keep these thoughts in your head as you go about preparing the lamb—the ritual of stuffing and securing with skewers. Focus on the color—tiny specks of tomatoes, wild rice, and parsley—how do they light up the meat and add a sense of occasion?

2 Artichoke hearts are a delicacy so take the time to study their unusual shape and texture. Look and compare each layer. How do the intricate centers compare to the rough exterior? As the roast begins to cook, do you feel a sense of familiarity and comfort? What memories does it evoke? Do they give off an aroma?

3 In a relaxed atmosphere with others, we often eat more than we really need. To avoid this, start eating only when everyone else at the table has begun. This will help you to slow down from the outset. Listen more and talk less, so you can concentrate on eating slowly. Tune in with another person who eats slowly. Follow his or her speed. Enjoy more and eat less.

Lamb stuffed with rice & peppers

Calories per serving 412
(not including roast potatoes)
Serves 4
Preparation time 40 minutes
Cooking time 1 hour 20 minutes

2 red bell peppers, cored, seeded, and halved
¼ cup wild rice, cooked
5 garlic cloves, chopped
5 semidried tomatoes, chopped
2 tablespoons chopped flat-leaf parsley
1¼ lb boneless leg of lamb, butterflied
4 artichoke halves
salt and pepper

Put the pepper halves in a roasting pan and cook in a preheated oven, 350°F, for 20 minutes until the skin has blackened and blistered. Cover with damp paper towels and set aside. When the peppers are cool enough to handle, peel off the skin and chop the flesh. (Leave the oven on.)

Mix together 1 of the chopped peppers, the rice, garlic, tomatoes, and parsley. Season to taste.

Put the lamb on a board and make a horizontal incision, almost all the way along, to make a cavity for stuffing. Fold back the top half, spoon in the stuffing, and fold back the top. Secure with skewers. Cook the lamb for 1 hour, basting frequently and adding the artichokes and other pepper for the last 15 minutes of cooking time. Slice the lamb and serve immediately with roasted new potatoes, if desired.

Asian chicken cakes

Calories per serving 213
(not including rice noodle salad)
Serves 4
Preparation time 15 minutes
Cooking time 16 minutes

1¼ lb ground chicken
1 lemon grass stalk, very finely chopped
2 kaffir lime leaves, very finely chopped
2 inch piece of fresh ginger root, peeled
and very finely chopped
2 green chiles, very finely chopped
2 garlic cloves, very finely chopped
1 egg, beaten
1 tablespoon sesame seeds, toasted

To serve
sweet chili dipping sauce
rice noodle salad with chopped
peanuts, sliced onion, bean sprouts,
and chopped fresh cilantro (optional)

Place the chicken in a large bowl with the lemon grass, kaffir lime leaves, ginger, chiles, and garlic, which need to be so finely chopped as to almost make a paste. Add the beaten egg and sesame seeds. Mix well, using your hands.

Heat a ridged grill pan or skillet. Divide the mixture into 16 and shape into small patties. Cook for 8 minutes on each side until cooked through.

Serve the chicken cakes with sweet chili dipping sauce and a salad of rice noodles, chopped peanuts, sliced onion, bean sprouts, and chopped cilantro, if desired.

AWARENESS POINTS

- Try and find a local Asian grocery store to get the most aromatic kaffir lime leaves on offer. If you nibble on a dried leaf, can you detect a bitterness around the stalk?
- The lemon grass stalk should feel firm and heavy if it is fresh—it may have dried out if it is too light. As you chop the lemon grass notice the woodlike texture.
- Notice the crunch of the peanuts and bean sprouts— how do the soft rice noodles offset this?

Baked fish with lemon grass

Calories per serving 284
(not including rice or vegetables)
Serves 4
Preparation time 10 minutes
Cooking time 20–25 minutes

2 lb whole fish (such as mackerel, sea bream, or sea bass), cleaned and scaled (if necessary) and scored 3–4 times with a sharp knife

4 x 5 inch lemon grass stalks, cut diagonally into 1 inch lengths

2 carrots, cut into matchsticks

4 tablespoons light soy sauce

2 tablespoons lime juice

1 red chile, finely chopped, plus extra slices to serve

To garnish
cilantro leaves
a few wedges of lemon, to serve

AWARENESS POINTS

- Always source your fish ethically.
- Taste the light soy sauce mindfully. How is dark soy sauce different?
- Eat slowly, taking time to appreciate how the tender fish melts on your tongue.

Place the fish in a baking dish and sprinkle with the lemon grass, carrots, 1½ tablespoons of the light soy sauce, and the lime juice.

Cover the baking dish with aluminum foil and bake in a preheated oven, 350°F, for 20–25 minutes or until the tip of a knife will slide easily into the flesh and come out clean. Place the fish on a warm serving plate and spoon over the sauce. Garnish with cilantro leaves and chile and serve with the lemon wedges.

Spoon the remaining light soy sauce into a small bowl with the chile and serve separately. Serve with other dishes, with boiled rice or on its own as a light meal with stir-fried or steamed vegetables.

Smoked mustard chicken

Calories per serving 345
(not including broccoli)
Serves 4
Preparation time 10 minutes
Cooking time 20 minutes

1 tablespoon wholegrain mustard
1 tablespoon extra-virgin olive oil
4 skinned and boneless chicken breasts,
   about 6 oz each
¾ cup uncooked rice
3 oz Earl Grey tea leaves
salt and pepper

For the salsa verde
handful of flat-leaf parsley
handful of mint leaves
handful of basil leaves
1 teaspoon capers
2 anchovies in oil
1 garlic clove, crushed
4 tablespoons olive oil
1 tablespoon red wine vinegar

AWARENESS POINTS
- Appreciate the process of smoking chicken from scratch. Celebrate that you have learned a new skill.
- What is more sour tasting— the capers or the anchovies?
- Enjoy blending the aromatic ingredients of salsa verde, noting how the smell increases when the herbs are crushed.

Stir together the mustard and extra-vrigin olive oil in a bowl and season with salt and pepper. Rub this mixture all over the chicken breasts and set aside.

Prepare a wok for smoking by lining it with aluminum foil, then add the rice and tea leaves, mixed together. Place a circular rack in the wok and place the wok over high heat with the lid on. Heat until smoke starts to escape out of it.

Remove the lid and quickly sit the chicken on the rack. Replace the lid and cook for 3 minutes, then reduce the heat to medium and cook for another 10 minutes. Turn the heat off and let the chicken sit in the wok for another 5 minutes while you prepare the salsa verde.

Blend all the salsa verde ingredients in a mini food processor or chop them up finely by hand. Put into a bowl and adjust the seasoning to taste. Serve the chicken warm or at room temperature with the salsa verde on the side and steamed vegetables such as tenderstem broccoli, if desired.

Quick prosciutto & arugula pizza

Calories per serving 498

Serves 4

Preparation time 10 minutes

Cooking time 10 minutes

4 mini pizza bases

2 garlic cloves, halved

8 oz reduced-fat mozzarella cheese, shredded

8 cherry tomatoes, quartered

5 oz prosciutto, sliced

2 oz arugula leaves, washed

balsamic vinegar, to taste

salt and pepper

Rub the top surfaces of the pizza bases with the cut faces of the garlic cloves. Transfer the bases to a baking sheet, top with mozzarella and tomatoes, and bake in a preheated oven, 400°F, for 10 minutes until the bread is golden.

Top the pizzas with slices of prosciutto and arugula leaves, season to taste with salt, pepper, and balsamic vinegar, and serve immediately.

AWARENESS POINTS

- Notice how the garlic juice feels on your fingertips.
- Consider how the smell of baking pizza makes you feel— excited, cozy, warm?
- Top your pizza decoratively, thinking about colors and shapes.

Roast pork with fennel

Calories per serving 451

Serves 4

Preparation time 10 minutes

Cooking time 30 minutes

1¼ lb pork tenderloin

1 large rosemary sprig, broken into short lengths, plus extra sprigs to garnish

3 garlic cloves, sliced

4 tablespoons olive oil

1 large fennel bulb, trimmed and cut into wedges, central core removed

1 large red onion, cut into wedges

1 large red bell pepper, cored, seeded, and cut into chunks

⅔ cup white wine

⅓ cup mascarpone cheese (optional)

salt and pepper

AWARENESS POINTS

- Take the time to position the rosemary sprigs and garlic evenly—the more nooks and crannies you cover, the more fragrant the meat will be.

- Fennel is an acquired taste—note the sweet anise flavor. Are there other similar-tasting ingredients you like or dislike?

- Taste the pork meat, looking for specific parts where the rosemary and garlic have infused the flesh.

Pierce the pork with a sharp knife and insert the pieces of rosemary and garlic evenly all over the tenderloin. Heat half the oil in a roasting pan on the stove, add the pork, and cook for 5 minutes or until browned all over.

Add the fennel, onion, and red pepper to the roasting pan and drizzle the vegetables with the remaining oil. Season well with salt and pepper. Roast in a preheated oven, 450°F, for 20 minutes or until the juices run clear when the pork is pierced in the center with a knife.

Transfer the pork and vegetables to a serving plate and keep hot in the oven. Add the wine to the roasting pan and simmer on the stove until slightly reduced. Stir in the mascarpone, if using.

Cut the pork into slices and arrange on 4 serving plates with spoonfuls of the roasted vegetables and a spoonful or two of the sauce. Serve immediately, garnished with rosemary sprigs.

Beef tenderloin with red pepper crust

Calories per serving 302
  (not including wholegrain rice)
Serves 4
Preparation time 15 minutes
Cooking time about 30 minutes

1 red bell pepper, halved and seeded
2 garlic cloves
8 dry black olives, pitted
1 tablespoon olive oil
2 teaspoons capers
8 shallots, peeled
scant ¼ cup balsamic vinegar
1 teaspoon light brown sugar
4 beef tenderloin steaks, about
  5 oz each
salt and pepper

AWARENESS POINTS

- Notice the changing texture of the pepper: from crunchy to soft to blended.
- Taste the rich, meaty beef and note what the sweet onions add to the experience.
- Really think about how hungry you are: can you serve a small spoonful of rice? Do you need rice at all?

Cook the red bell pepper under a preheated hot broiler until the skin blackens. Remove and cover with damp paper towels until it is cool enough to handle, then peel the skin off and chop.

In a food processor, blend together the garlic, olives, 1 teaspoon of the oil, the capers, and the chopped red bell pepper.

Put the shallots and the remaining oil in a small pan. Cover and cook over low heat for 15 minutes, stirring frequently. Add the vinegar and sugar and cook uncovered for another 5 minutes, stirring frequently.

Meanwhile, season the steaks and cook, 2 at a time, in a preheated heavy skillet or ridged grill pan. Cook on one side for 2 minutes, then transfer to a baking sheet. Top each steak with some red pepper mix. Bake in a preheated oven, 400°F, for 5 minutes or according to taste. Let rest in a warm place for 5 minutes before serving with the balsamic shallots and, if desired, steamed wholegrain rice and arugula leaves.

Haddock packages & coconut rice

Calories per serving 340

Serves 4

Preparation time 15 minutes

Cooking time 20 minutes

4 haddock fillets, about
   5 oz each

4 tablespoons chopped fresh cilantro

1 red chile, chopped

1 shallot, finely sliced

1 lime, sliced, plus extra lime halves
   to serve

2 lemon grass stalks, 1 coarsely
   chopped and 1 bashed

1 cup Thai jasmine rice

1¾ cups water

2 fresh or dried kaffir lime leaves

scant ¼ cup reduced-fat coconut milk

AWARENESS POINTS

- Slice your ingredients delicately to suit the delicate flavors—the cilantro and shallots should be as prominent as the strong chile and lime.

- Arrange the packages with care so that they will be attractive when opened—think of the process like wrapping a present.

- Savor the smells of warm, exotic lemon grass and coconut. How does the milk change the consistency of the rice? Does this wetter texture increase your appetite?

Cut 4 pieces of nonstick parchment paper, each 12 inches square. Put a haddock fillet in the center of each piece and arrange some of the cilantro, chile, shallot, lime, and chopped lemon grass stalk evenly over each. Wrap them up into neat packages.

Transfer the packages to a baking sheet and cook in a preheated oven, 350°F, for 20 minutes until the fish is cooked through.

Meanwhile, put the rice in a pan with the water, the bashed lemon grass stalk and the lime leaves. Cover and simmer for 12 minutes. When the rice is cooked and the water absorbed, stir in the coconut milk. Serve with the haddock packages, with some extra lime halves.

Lemon grass chicken

Calories per serving 476

Serves 4

Preparation time 15 minutes

Cooking time 1¾–2¼ hours

1 tablespoon sunflower oil

12 large chicken drumsticks (remove
    skin before eating)

1 onion, finely chopped

4 garlic cloves, crushed

6 tablespoons very finely chopped
    lemon grass and 1 lemon grass stalk,
    halved lengthwise

1 red chile, finely sliced or chopped

2 tablespoons medium curry paste

1 tablespoon grated palm sugar

1 cup chicken stock

salt and pepper

AWARENESS POINTS

- See if you can buy organic chicken.
- Enjoy the slow cooking process and take this time to pursue a hobby or meditate.
- Mark the way the tender chicken falls from the bone and "melts" as you eat it.

Heat the oil in a large, heavy casserole dish and brown the drumsticks evenly for 5–6 minutes. Remove with a slotted spoon and set aside.

Add the onion and stir-fry over low heat for 10 minutes. Add the garlic, chopped lemon grass, chile, and curry paste and stir-fry for 1–2 minutes.

Return the chicken to the dish with the palm sugar and stock. Bring to a boil, season, and cover tightly. Cook in a preheated oven, 275°F, for 1½–2 hours or until tender and cooked through. Remove from the oven and serve immediately.

Okra & coconut stew

Calories per serving 421

Serves 4

Preparation time 15 minutes

Cooking time 40 minutes

12 oz okra

4 tablespoons vegetable oil

2 onions, chopped

2 green bell peppers, cored, seeded,
    and cut into chunks

3 celery stalks, thinly sliced

3 garlic cloves, crushed

4 teaspoons Cajun spice blend

½ teaspoon ground turmeric

1½ cups vegetable stock

1¾ cups can coconut milk

1½ cups frozen corn

juice of 1 lime

4 tablespoons chopped fresh cilantro

salt and pepper

Trim the stalk ends from the okra and cut the pods into ¾ inch lengths.

Heat 2 tablespoons of the oil in a large deep-sided skillet or shallow ovenproof casserole and fry the okra for 5 minutes. Lift out with a slotted spoon onto a plate.

Add the remaining oil to the pan and very gently fry the onions, peppers, and celery for 10 minutes until softened but not browned, stirring frequently. Add the garlic, spice blend, and turmeric and cook for 1 minute.

Pour in the stock and coconut milk and bring to a boil. Reduce the heat, cover, and cook gently for 10 minutes. Return the okra to the pan with the corn, lime juice, and cilantro and cook for another 10 minutes. Season to taste with salt and pepper and serve.

AWARENESS POINTS

- Note the intricacy of the okra—the tessellated pattern and ridged shape.
- Mark the deep yellow of the turmeric. Be careful of it staining your hands and white crockery.
- Enjoy delving into the stew with its many textures and layers.

Eggplant packages with pine nuts

Calories per serving 436

Serves 2

Preparation time 30 minutes, plus chilling

Cooking time 12–15 minutes

1 tablespoon pine nuts

1 long, large eggplant

4 oz mozzarella cheese

1 large or 2 small plum tomatoes

8 large basil leaves, plus extra, torn, to garnish

1 tablespoon olive oil

salt and pepper

Tomato dressing

2 tablespoons olive oil

1 teaspoon balsamic vinegar

1 teaspoon tomato paste

1 teaspoon lemon juice

Make the dressing. Whisk together the oil, vinegar, tomato paste, and lemon juice in a small bowl. Set aside.

Dry-fry the pine nuts in a hot pan until golden brown. Remove from the pan and set aside.

Cut the stalk off the eggplant and cut it lengthwise to give 8 slices (disregarding the ends). Cook the slices in a saucepan of boiling salted water for 2 minutes. Drain and dry on paper towels. Cut the mozzarella into 4 slices and the tomato into 8 slices (disregarding the outer edges).

Put 2 eggplant slices in an ovenproof dish, forming an X-shape. Put a slice of tomato on top, season with salt and pepper, add a basil leaf, a slice of mozzarella, another basil leaf, then more salt and pepper, and finally another slice of tomato. Fold the edges of the eggplant around the filling to make a package. Repeat with the other ingredients to make 4 packages in total. Cover and chill in the refrigerator for 20 minutes.

Brush the eggplant packages with the oil. Put the dish under a preheated hot broiler and cook for about 5 minutes on each side until golden-brown. Serve 2 packages per person, drizzled with the dressing, and sprinkled with the pine nuts and torn basil leaves.

AWARENESS POINTS

- Explore the rubbery texture of the mozzarella. Do you know how it is made?
- Pay attention to the tightness of the packages and the layers inside—neat and even will get best results.
- You may find that your technique gets better as you go along so don't be critical.

Chicken with orange & mint

Calories per serving 355
(not including couscous)

Serves 4

Preparation time 5 minutes

Cooking time 15–20 minutes

4 boneless, skinless chicken breasts,
about 7 oz each

3 tablespoons olive oil

⅔ cup freshly squeezed
orange juice

1 small orange, sliced

2 tablespoons chopped mint

1 tablespoon butter

salt and pepper

AWARENESS POINTS

- Buy organic chicken and know
  your food source.
- Smell the fresh mint and the
  citrus tang of orange.
- Take slow bites and consider
  the mix of flavors—can you
  taste each one?

Season the chicken breasts to taste with salt and pepper.
Heat the oil in a large nonstick skillet, add the chicken
breasts, and cook over medium heat for 4–5 minutes or
until golden all over, turning once.

Pour in the orange juice, add the orange slices, and bring
to a gentle simmer. Cover tightly, reduce the heat to low,
and cook gently for 8–10 minutes or until the chicken
is cooked through. Add the chopped mint and butter
and stir to mix well. Cook over high heat, stirring, for
2 minutes. Serve with couscous, if desired.

Guided practice

The soup in the first recipe here combines chunks of delicious squash with protein-rich beans and bright green, vitamin-rich kale. Its liquid stock and its vegetable content mean that the body will be refreshed by fluids, as well as food nutrients.

1 Vegetables can be the key ingredients of light meals, suitable for summertime or lunches on the go, but they can also be combined to create comforting, satisfying dishes. Sweet potatoes, butternut squash, and root vegetables, such as rutabaga or carrots, can be roasted or used in hearty stews and soups. Green vegetables provide a bitter and refreshing flavor contrast, and are packed full of iron and vitamin C, essential for a healthy body. Beans are cheap to buy, and provide a great, low-fat way of taking in protein and fiber, perfect for achieving and keeping the feeling of a full stomach, and healthy digestion.

2 Appreciate the changing aromas as the onion, garlic, and spices fry together when you begin cooking. Notice the subtle changes as you add ingredients. As the combined ingredients cook, notice that their juices blend with the stock to swell the soup, even as some liquid bubbles away in the cooking process.

3 Taste the soup carefully, testing the seasoning as you go. Check the texture of the vegetables—perhaps you prefer them with a bit of crunch. Let it cool gently before you begin to eat it. Use a wide, flat spoon, and sip the liquid slowly, taking care to chew the vegetables and paying attention to way the soup's warmth affects how your body feels.

Squash, kale & mixed bean soup

Calories per serving 182
(not including garlic bread)
Serves 6
Preparation time 15 minutes
Cooking time 45 minutes

1 tablespoon olive oil
1 onion, finely chopped
2 garlic cloves, finely chopped
1 teaspoon smoked paprika
1 lb butternut squash, halved,
    seeded, peeled, and diced
2 small carrots, peeled and diced
1 lb tomatoes, skinned (optional)
    and coarsely chopped
1 (13 oz) can mixed beans,
    rinsed and drained
3½ cups hot vegetable stock
⅔ cup half-fat crème fraîche
3½ oz kale, torn
    into bite-size pieces
salt and pepper

Heat the oil in a saucepan over medium-low heat, add the onion, and fry gently for 5 minutes. Stir in the garlic and smoked paprika and cook briefly, then add the squash, carrots, tomatoes, and mixed beans.

Pour in the stock, season with salt and pepper, and bring to a boil, stirring frequently. Reduce the heat, cover, and simmer for 25 minutes or until the vegetables are cooked and tender.

Stir in the crème fraîche, then add the kale, pressing it just beneath the surface of the stock. Cover and cook for 5 minutes or until the kale has just wilted. Ladle into bowls and serve with warm garlic bread, if desired.

Salmon curry with tomato salad

Calories per serving 477

Serves 2

Preparation time 10 minutes

Cooking time 20–25 minutes

1 teaspoon vegetable oil

1 small onion, sliced

1 garlic clove, chopped

1 teaspoon tandoori spice mix

1 cinnamon stick

5 oz cherry tomatoes, halved

4 tablespoons reduced-fat crème fraîche

grated zest and juice of ½ lime

6 oz skinless salmon fillet, cut into chunks

1 tablespoon chopped mint

1 tablespoon chopped fresh cilantro

Tomato & onion salad

5 oz vine-ripened tomatoes, thinly sliced

1 small red onion, finely sliced

handful of fresh cilantro, chopped

1 teaspoon lemon juice

Heat the oil in a small skillet, add the onion and garlic, and fry for 2–3 minutes until softened. Stir in the spice mix and cinnamon stick and fry for another 1 minute. Add the tomatoes, crème fraîche, lime zest, and juice and heat for 1 minute.

Put the salmon in an ovenproof dish. Spoon over the sauce, cover the dish tightly with foil, and cook in a preheated oven, 400°F, for 15–20 minutes or until the salmon is just cooked through.

Meanwhile, make the salad. Toss together the tomatoes, onion, and cilantro, and dress with lemon juice. Serve the salmon with the tomato and onion salad.

AWARENESS POINTS

- Make sure your salmon is from a sustainable source. Adapt the recipe with a sustainable fish if not.
- Choose the sweetest, reddest tomatoes for the fullest flavor.
- Taste the sauce before and after the crème fraîche and notice the changes.

Lentil moussaka

Calories per serving 304

Serves 4

Preparation time 10 minutes

Cooking time 45–50 minutes,
   plus standing

½ cup dried brown or green lentils,
   rinsed and drained

1 (13 oz) can chopped tomatoes

2 garlic cloves, crushed

½ teaspoon dried oregano

pinch of ground nutmeg

⅔ cup vegetable stock,
   plus extra if needed

2–3 tablespoons vegetable oil

8 oz eggplant, sliced

1 onion, finely chopped

Cheese topping

1 egg

⅔ cup soft cheese

pinch of ground nutmeg

salt and pepper

Put the lentils in a saucepan with the tomatoes, garlic, oregano, and nutmeg. Pour in the stock. Bring to a boil, then reduce the heat and simmer for 20 minutes until the lentils are tender but not mushy, topping off with extra stock as needed.

Meanwhile, heat the oil in a skillet and lightly fry the eggplant and onion until the onion is soft and the eggplant is golden on both sides.

Layer the eggplant mixture and lentil mixture alternately in an ovenproof dish.

Make the topping. In a bowl, beat together the egg, cheese, and nutmeg with a good dash of salt and pepper. Pour over the moussaka and cook in a preheated oven, 400°F, for 20–25 minutes. Remove from the oven and let stand for 5 minutes before serving with salad greens.

AWARENESS POINTS

- Appreciate nutmeg as a powerful ingredient —the Chinese used it for inflammation, the Roman civilizations used it for stress relief, and it has been known to ease indigestion.
- Enjoy the contrasting layers in the slices of moussaka—does it feel like a richer, more filling meal?
- Serve small portions, and eat slowly: lentils and eggs are filling foods.

Chicken wrapped in prosciutto

Calories per serving 431

Serves 4

Preparation time 10 minutes

Cooking time about 10 minutes

4 boneless, skinless chicken breasts,
about 5 oz each

4 slices of prosciutto

4 sage leaves

all-purpose flour, for dusting

2 tablespoons butter

2 tablespoons olive oil

4 sprigs cherry tomatoes on the vine

⅔ cup dry white wine

salt and pepper

AWARENESS POINTS

- Notice the smell and texture of sage leaves—how downy are they?
- How do the sweet cherry tomatoes contrast the salty ham?
- This is a great example of using awareness to ensure your chicken is safe and fully cooked—make sure the juices run clear.

Lay each chicken breast between 2 sheets of plastic wrap and flatten with a rolling pin or meat mallet until wafer thin. Season with salt and pepper.

Lay a slice of prosciutto on each chicken breast, followed by a sage leaf. Secure the sage and ham in position with a toothpick, then lightly dust both sides of the chicken with flour. Season again with salt and pepper.

Heat the butter and oil in a large skillet over high heat, add the chicken, and cook for 4–5 minutes on each side or until the juices run clear when pierced with a knife. Add the tomatoes and wine to the pan and bubble until the wine has thickened and reduced by about half. Serve immediately, accompanied by a green salad.

Chili pork with pineapple rice

Calories per serving 440

Serves 4

Preparation time 20 minutes,
   plus marinating

Cooking time 15 minutes

2 tablespoons sunflower oil
2 tablespoons lime juice
2 garlic cloves, crushed
1 red chile, seeded and finely chopped
10 oz pork tenderloin, cubed
1 cup Thai fragrant rice
6 scallions, finely sliced
7 oz pineapple, peeled and diced
½ red onion, cut into wedges
1 lime, cut into wedges
salt and pepper
ready-made sweet chili sauce, to serve

Presoak 8 wooden skewers in warm water. Mix together the oil, lime juice, garlic, chile, and salt and pepper in a bowl, add the pork, and stir to coat. Cover and let marinate in the refrigerator for at least 1 hour.

Cook the rice in lightly salted boiling water for 12–15 minutes or according to the directions on the package. Drain and stir through the scallions and pineapple.

Meanwhile, thread the pork onto the skewers, alternating it with onion and lime wedges, and cook under a preheated hot broiler for about 10 minutes, turning frequently and basting with the remaining marinade, until the pork is cooked through.

Put the skewers and rice on a plate with the sweet chili sauce and serve immediately.

AWARENESS POINTS
- Load your skewers with an eye to the visual—make a pattern.
- Taste the dish mindfully, noting sweet and sour in turn.
- Serve the sauce in a favorite bowl or saucer.

Malaysian rendang lamb

Calories per serving 455

Serves 6

Preparation time 15 minutes, plus standing

Cooking time 2¾ hours

2 tablespoons sunflower oil

1¾ lb leg of lamb, butterflied

2 onions, finely chopped

1 tablespoon ground coriander

1 teaspoon ground turmeric

6 garlic cloves, crushed

6 tablespoons very finely chopped lemon grass

4–6 bird's eye chiles, chopped

4 tablespoons finely chopped fresh cilantro root and stem

1 (14 oz) can reduced-fat coconut milk

salt and pepper

Heat the oil in a deep, heavy casserole dish and brown the lamb on both sides for about 5–6 minutes.

Place the remaining ingredients in a food processor and blend until smooth. Season well.

Pour this mixture over the lamb and bring to a boil. Cover tightly and place in a preheated oven at 300°F, for 2½ hours, turning occasionally, until the lamb is meltingly tender and most of the liquid has evaporated.

Remove from the oven and let stand for about 10–12 minutes before serving, cut into thick slices.

AWARENESS POINTS

- This can be a very impressive dish to serve to friends. Think about who you would like to treat.
- Allow the recommended full cooking and standing time, build up to a sense of occasion, let your appetite reach a healthy level and your mind unwind from any emotional stress.
- Notice the melting, tender texture of each mouthful of lamb.

Seafood & vegetable stir-fry

Calories per serving 220
(not including the rice)

Serves 4

Preparation time 20 minutes

Cooking time 7–10 minutes

8 oz live mussels

8 oz water chestnuts, peeled
and thickly sliced

1 tablespoon superfine sugar

½ teaspoon black pepper

2 tablespoons vegetable oil

1 sweet white onion, sliced

4 oz raw peeled tiger shrimp

4 scallions, diagonally sliced

½ teaspoon crushed red pepper flakes,
plus extra to garnish

4 oz sugar snap peas, trimmed and
diagonally halved

1¼ cups bean sprouts

3 tablespoons light soy sauce

2 tablespoons yellow bean sauce

2 tablespoons Chinese rice wine
or dry sherry

chervil sprigs, to garnish

AWARENESS POINTS

- Vary your vegetables according
  to season and source locally.
- Inhale and appreciate the hot,
  spicy steam from your wok.
- Enjoy the contrast of the
  softly chewy mussels and the
  crunchy veg.

Scrub the mussels thoroughly under cold running water. Pull off the hairy "beards" and rinse again. Gently tap any open mussels and discard any that do not close.

Sprinkle the water chestnuts with the sugar and pepper and set aside.

Heat the oil in a wok over high heat until the oil starts to shimmer. Add the onion and mussels and stir-fry quickly for 1 minute. Put a lid on the wok and cook for 3–4 minutes or until the mussels have opened. Discard any mussels that remain closed.

Add the water chestnuts, shrimp, scallions, red pepper flakes, sugar snaps, and bean sprouts to the wok and stir-fry for 1–2 minutes or until the shrimp have turned pink and are cooked through.

Mix together the soy sauce, yellow bean sauce, and rice wine or sherry and pour over the ingredients in the wok. Stir-fry for another 1–2 minutes until hot. Garnish with red pepper flakes and chervil sprigs. Serve with rice.

Mushroom stroganoff

Calories per serving 239
Serves 4
Preparation time 10 minutes
Cooking time 10 minutes

1 tablespoon butter
2 tablespoons olive oil
1 onion, thinly sliced
4 garlic cloves, finely chopped
1 lb cremini mushrooms, sliced
2 tablespoons wholegrain mustard
1 cup half-fat crème fraîche
salt and pepper
3 tablespoons chopped parsley,
    to garnish

Heat the butter and oil in a large skillet,
add the onion and garlic, and cook until soft and
starting to brown.

Add the mushrooms to the pan and cook until soft
and starting to brown. Stir in the mustard and crème
fraîche and just heat through. Season to taste with
salt and pepper, then serve immediately, garnished
with the chopped parsley.

AWARENESS POINTS
- Taste the wholegrain mustard and mark the sweetness and heat. How does it compare to English or American mustard?
- Notice the satisfying, meaty texture of the mushrooms.
- This recipe is incredibly simple to make—how will you spend the extra time?

Burmese chicken noodle curry

Calories per serving 403

Serves 6

Preparation time 20 minutes

Cooking time about 1 hour

2 lb boneless, skinless chicken thighs, cut into bite-size pieces

2 onions, chopped

5 garlic cloves, chopped

1 teaspoon peeled and finely grated fresh ginger root

2 tablespoons sunflower oil

½ teaspoon Burmese shrimp paste (belacan)

1 (14 oz) can coconut milk

1 tablespoon medium curry powder

10½ oz dried rice vermicelli

salt and pepper

To garnish

chopped fresh cilantro

finely chopped red onion

fried garlic slivers

sliced fresh red chiles

lime wedges

Season the chicken pieces and set aside. Process the onion, garlic, and ginger in a food processor until smooth. If necessary, add a little water to assist in blending the mixture. Heat the oil in a large pan. Add the onion mixture and shrimp paste and cook, stirring, over high heat for about 5 minutes.

Add the chicken and cook over medium heat, turning it until it browns.

Pour in the coconut milk and add the curry powder. Bring to a boil, reduce the heat, cover, and simmer, covered, for about 30 minutes, stirring occasionally. Uncover the pan and cook for another 15 minutes or until the chicken is tender and cooked through.

Meanwhile, place the noodles in a bowl, cover with boiling water, and set aside for 10 minutes. Drain the noodles and divide them between 4 large warmed serving bowls. Ladle over the curry, and garnish with chopped cilantro, chopped red onion, fried garlic slivers, sliced red chiles, and lime wedges.

AWARENESS POINTS

- Buy cage-free organic chicken thighs if you can.
- Shrimp paste can be extremely pungent—note how the smell diffuses after cooking.
- Be slow and meticulous in finely slicing your garnishes.

Mindful treats

Guilt food—how to deal with cravings

This book is based on the idea that behind every weight problem is a human being. Most of us have dieted or have seen friends losing and gaining weight. Most diets don't work because they deal with food intake only, not with the human being who consumes it. We gain weight because we eat when we are not hungry; we become too thin when we deprive ourselves of food when we do need it. In both cases, the mind overrides simple body symptoms and tries to solve unpleasant moods and feelings by eating, or not eating.

We all look for quick solutions to our inner dissatisfactions by seeking satisfying experiences through food. Unfortunately, this doesn't work. We can get satisfaction through food when we are hungry, but we can't feed the longings of our mind with food. We have to learn to differentiate between the needs of our body and the needs and desires of our mind and soul.

In this exercise you will gain more insight into the triggers that make you eat even when you are not hungry. As you become more aware of the moments before you fall into your unhelpful eating pattern, you will find it easier to change it. You will slowly unlock the origin of dissatisfaction and hurt that is keeping these thinking and behavior patterns in place. Having done this, you can start to find other ways—developing new neuro pathways—of dealing with unhappiness and pain.

A WEEK WITHOUT

Try giving up any one of the following for a week, and explore the experience:

sugar
snacks
your favorite caffeine
dairy food
white flour
alcohol
meat
prepacked food
complaining
internet
cell phone
car

The flesh is willing ... what are your food triggers?

The point of this exercise is to become more aware of what happens just prior to indulging in food or drink, to help you spot the most irresistible triggers.

• Begin by putting your hand on your heart or solar plexus and visualizing being cradled by overflowing compassion. You may want to see somebody who symbolizes kindness for you.

• Review how your overeating or undereating has harmed you and others, and think about how you would like to change this destructive pattern.

• Help your mind to slow down and relax by bringing awareness to your breathing for a little while.

• Fill your mind with care and compassion, and the will to transform your behavior. Allow yourself to be nurtured by this energy.

• Then shift your memory to the last time you overindulged in food. Recall the moment it started, and then go back an instant to when you were just about to start engaging in your addictive behavior. Contemplate what was occurring during that moment. Find out what this starting point feels like.

• Try to bring vivid awareness to your surroundings at that time. Imagine this is all happening right now. Can you see yourself and where you are? Are there any people nearby or are you alone? What odors are present? What tastes do you notice in your mouth and what sounds can you hear? Is your body sensitive or numb? Are you physically and mentally comfortable or uncomfortable?

Any of these factors could be an external trigger. View it with composure and slight detachment, as you would look at a photograph or as if you were a CCTV camera just filming but not reacting to what is recorded.

• Carry on deepening your awareness of what was occurring at that time. Were you in any pain? Did you feel stressed? Were you trying to calm down? Had you just been involved in an argument? Did you feel lonesome? Had someone upset you or had you frustrated yourself? Were you trying to impress anyone? Did life feel disappointing? Was it difficult to cope?

Any of these could have been internal triggers. View them peacefully and with kindness. Remain aware of that moment as long as you possibly can. Pinpoint those factors that set you off. Accept that this is your current reality, and is the way in which you cope with difficulties for now.

Guided practice

Everything in moderation. There are many ways to celebrate food and the act of having something to eat as a reward can be interpreted with a more mindful approach. For example, rather than assuming an unhealthy chocolate cake will boost your mood or transform your stressful day, stop and think about what you actually need. Be true to your body's signals and sensations. It may be that you need to drink more water or boost low blood sugar. In this book, there is no suggestion of giving up your favorite foods and indulgences; simply widen your perception when it comes to treating yourself with food. Is there a healthier alternative? Can you give up caffeine for a week and explore the experience? And when you do treat yourself with food, are you getting the most out of it—savoring every taste sensation rather than eating on autopilot?

1 The first recipe here, for chocolate Florentines, is a perfect example of eating something very decadent and delicious in moderation. One Florentine is crammed with textures and flavors to enjoy—slivered almonds, candied peel, rich dark chocolate. One tiny Florentine can contain a wealth of treats. The trick, of course, is to be mindful and not eat the whole lot!

2 When you add the dried ingredients, one by one, into the melted sugar and butter mixture, notice how different and wonderful they are—a cascade of coarsely chopped candied cherries, tumbling hazelnuts, small crystals of candied peel. There are hundreds of combinations of dried fruit and nuts to try.

3 As you spoon the mixture carefully onto the baking sheets, listen to the crackling of paper and notice the stickiness.

4 Notice the texture of the thin layer of precious, rich, dark chocolate as you spread it on the Florentines.

5 Finally, when you come to eat your compact treat, notice the different sweet tastes and textures with every nibble—the sharpness of the candied peel, the smooth, sweet but bitter chocolate and the crunchy almond slivers. See if you can make a list of 10–20 different sensations. Read it back to yourself and see how one treat can be enhanced with a complex, mindful approach.

Florentines

Calories per serving 126
Makes 26
Preparation time 20 minutes, plus cooling
Cooking time 20–25 minutes

7 tablespoons butter
½ cup superfine sugar
3 oz multicolored candied cherries,
   coarsely chopped
¾ cup slivered almonds
2 oz whole candied peel, finely chopped
⅓ cup hazelnuts, coarsely chopped
2 tablespoons all-purpose flour
5 oz semisweet chocolate,
   broken into pieces

Put the butter and sugar in a saucepan and heat gently until the butter has melted and the sugar dissolved. Remove the pan from the heat and stir in all the remaining ingredients except the chocolate.

Spoon tablespoons of the mixture, well spaced apart, onto 3 baking sheets lined with nonstick parchment paper. Flatten the mounds slightly. Cook 1 baking sheet at a time in the center of a preheated oven, 350°F, for 5–7 minutes until the nuts are golden.

After removing each baking sheet from the oven, neaten and shape the cooked cookies by placing a slightly larger plain round cookie cutter over the top and rotating to smooth and tidy up the edges. Let cool.

Melt the chocolate in a heatproof bowl set over a saucepan of gently simmering water. Peel the cookies off the lining paper and arrange upside down on a wire rack. Spoon the melted chocolate over the flat underside of the cookies and spread the surfaces level. Let cool and harden.

Black forest brownies

Calories per serving 317
 (not including chocolate sauce)

Cuts into 12

Preparation time 25 minutes,
 plus cooling

Cooking time 25–30 minutes

9 tablespoons slightly salted butter,
 plus extra for greasing

5 oz semisweet chocolate, chopped

2 eggs

¾ cup packed dark brown sugar

1 teaspoon vanilla extract

¼ cup + 4 teaspoons all-purpose flour

½ teaspoon baking powder

7 oz black or red cherries, pitted and
 halved, plus extra to serve

To serve

⅔ cup heavy cream
chocolate shavings

Grease an 7 inch square cake pan or shallow baking pan and line it with nonstick parchment paper.

Melt 2 oz of the chocolate and the butter in a heatproof bowl set over a saucepan of gently simmering water (don't let the bottom of the bowl touch the water). Beat the eggs, sugar, and vanilla extract in a separate bowl until light and foamy. Stir in the melted chocolate mixture. Tip in the flour, baking powder, cherries, and remaining chocolate and mix together until combined.

Spoon the batter into the prepared pan and level the surface. Bake in a preheated oven, 350°F, for 20–25 minutes or until just firm to the touch. Let cool in the pan, then transfer to a board and peel off the lining paper.

Whip the cream in a bowl until peaking, then spread over the cake. Sprinkle with chocolate shavings and cut into small squares. Serve with extra cherries and rich chocolate sauce, if desired.

AWARENESS POINTS

- Spoil yourself in true childhood fashion—after you have transferred the melted chocolate to the mixing bowl, lick the spoon a couple of times before you wash it.

- Compare the consistency of the melted chocolate, foamy egg mixture, and the coarse combined mixture.

- Try and eat just one small square at a time—enjoy this a bite-size, balanced treat.

Mango & passion fruit brûlée

Calories per serving 202

Serves 4

Preparation time 10 minutes, plus chilling

Cooking time 1–2 minutes

1 small mango, peeled, seeded, and thinly sliced
2 passion fruit, flesh scooped out
1¼ cups low-fat plain yogurt
scant 1 cup half-fat crème fraîche
1 tablespoon confectioners' sugar
few drops of vanilla extract
2 tablespoons raw brown sugar

Arrange the mango slices in 4 ramekins.

Stir together the passion fruit flesh, yogurt, crème fraîche, confectioners' sugar, and vanilla extract in a bowl, then spoon the mixture over the mango. Tap each ramekin to level the surface.

Sprinkle over the raw brown sugar and cook the brûlées under a preheated hot broiler for 1–2 minutes until the sugar has melted. Chill for about 30 minutes, then serve.

For plum & peach brûlée, replace the mango with 2 sliced peaches. Continue as above, replacing the passion fruit with 4 firm but ripe chopped plums. Before broiling, top each ramekin with a piece of chopped candied ginger.

AWARENESS POINTS

- Notice the crack of the surface as you break into it.
- How does the sharp brittle texture feel on your tongue?
- Where in your mouth can you taste the passion fruit and vanilla?

Tuile baskets & strawberry cream

Calories per serving 404

Serves 6

Preparation time 40 minutes

Cooking time 15–18 minutes

2 egg whites

½ cup superfine sugar

3½ tablespoons unsalted butter, melted

few drops of vanilla extract

¼ cup + 4 teaspoons all-purpose flour

Strawberry cream

1 cup heavy cream

4 tablespoons confectioners' sugar, plus
  extra for dusting

2 tablespoons chopped mint,
  plus extra leaves to decorate

1¾ cups strawberries, hulled and
  halved or sliced, depending on size

AWARENESS POINTS

- Lay out the ingredients and savor the smell of the vanilla, mint, and strawberries in turn. Which affects your appetite the most?

- Making the pleats and shaping the tuiles is intricate work so allow yourself extra time—let it be it a calm activity.

- How does the mint contrast the sweetness of the sugar?

Put the egg whites in a bowl and break up with a fork. Stir in the superfine sugar, then the butter and vanilla extract. Sift in the flour and mix until smooth.

Drop 1 heaping tablespoon of the mixture onto a baking sheet lined with nonstick parchment paper. Drop a second spoonful well apart from the first, then spread each into a thin circle about 5 inches in diameter. Bake in a preheated oven, 375°F, for 5–6 minutes until just beginning to brown around the edges.

Add 2 more spoonfuls to a second paper-lined baking sheet and spread thinly. Remove the baked tuiles from the oven and put the second tray in. Leave the cooked tuiles to firm up for 5–10 seconds, then carefully lift them off the paper one at a time and drape each over an orange. Pinch the edges into pleats and let harden for 2–3 minutes, then carefully ease off. Repeat until 6 tuiles have been made.

Whip the cream lightly, then fold in the mint, the strawberries, and nearly all of the confectioners' sugar, setting aside 6 strawberry halves for the decoration. Spoon into the tuiles, then top with the mint leaves and the strawberry halves. Sift with the remaining confectioners' sugar.

Broiled fruits with palm sugar

Calories per serving 176
  (not including the ice cream)
Serves 4
Preparation time 10 minutes
Cooking time 6–16 minutes

2 tablespoons palm sugar
grated zest and juice of 1 lime
2 tablespoons water
½ teaspoon cracked black peppercorns
1 lb mixed prepared fruits, such as
  pineapple or peach slices or mango
  wedges

To serve
cinnamon or vanilla ice cream
lime slices

Put the sugar, lime zest and juice, measured water, and peppercorns in a small saucepan and heat over low heat until the sugar has dissolved. Plunge the bottom of the pan into iced water to cool.

Brush the cooled syrup over the prepared fruits and cook under a preheated hot broiler for 6–8 minutes on each side, or over a preheated hot gas barbecue or the hot coals of a charcoal barbecue, for 3–4 minutes on each side until charred and tender.

Serve with scoops of cinnamon or vanilla ice cream and lime slices.

For broiled fruit kebabs, cut the prepared fruits into large chunks, thread onto wooden skewers, presoaked in cold water for 30 minutes, and brush with the cooled syrup before cooking as in the recipe above.

AWARENESS POINTS

- Try a drop of lime juice—does your face react to the sharp taste? Do the same with a piece of peppercorn and compare your reaction? Which do you prefer and why?
- How many shades of orange and yellow can you find in the different prepared fruits? Do these colors brighten your mood?
- If you use a barbecue, does the smell of the coals evoke any memories? What about the smell of cinnamon or vanilla?

Pomegranate & ginger slice

Calories per serving 121

Cuts into 20

Preparation time 25 minutes

Cooking time 50 minutes

1⅔ cups all-purpose flour

1 teaspoon baking soda

scant ½ cup milk

1 egg

½ cup packed dark brown sugar

⅓ cup blackstrap molasses

5 tablespoons unsalted butter, plus
   extra for greasing

3 pieces of preserved ginger in syrup,
   chopped

Topping

1¼ cups pomegranate juice

2 tablespoons honey

1 pomegranate

AWARENESS POINTS

- Note how the molasses changes the consistency of the mixture and then changes again as it dissolves.
- Be mindful of your pantry ingredients. Jarred ginger can be reused to spice up juices and smoothies or make a batch of gingerbread.
- Appreciate the pop of bold color that the pomegranate adds to the dark brown bake.

Sift the flour and baking soda into a bowl. Beat together the milk and egg in a small bowl. Put the sugar, molasses, and butter in a saucepan and heat gently until the butter melts and the sugar dissolves. Remove from the heat and add to the milk mixture with the chopped ginger. Add to the dry ingredients and stir together using a large metal spoon until well combined.

Spoon the mixture into 2 greased and lined 2 lb loaf pans and level the surface. Bake in a preheated oven, 325°F, for 30 minutes or until just firm to the touch and a skewer inserted into the center comes out clean. Let cool in the pans, then loosen at the ends and transfer to a wire rack. Peel off the lining paper.

Make the topping. Pour the pomegranate juice into a saucepan and bring to a boil, then boil for about 15 minutes until thick and syrupy and reduced to about 3 tablespoons. Stir in the honey. Halve the pomegranate and push the halves inside out to release the fleshy seeds, discarding any white membrane. Sprinkle the seeds over the top of the cakes. Drizzle with the syrup and cut into 20 small squares to serve.

Chocolate, zucchini & nut cake

Calories per serving 266

Serves 12

Preparation time 10–15 minutes, plus cooling

Cooking time 40 minutes

8 oz zucchini, coarsely shredded

2 eggs

scant ½ cup vegetable oil, plus extra for greasing

grated zest and juice of 1 orange

⅔ cup superfine sugar

1¾ cups all-purpose flour

2 tablespoons unsweetened cocoa

½ teaspoon baking soda

1½ teaspoons baking powder

¼ cup ready-to-eat dried apricots, chopped

Topping

scant 1 cup cream cheese

2 tablespoons chocolate hazelnut spread

1 tablespoon hazelnuts, toasted and chopped

Place the zucchini in a strainer and squeeze out any excess liquid.

Beat together the eggs, oil, orange zest and juice, and sugar in a large bowl. Sift in the flour, cocoa, baking soda, and baking powder and beat to combine.

Fold in the zucchini and apricots, then spoon the batter into a greased and lined 8 inch deep loose-bottom cake pan.

Bake in a preheated oven, 350°F, for 40 minutes until risen and firm to the touch. Turn out onto a wire rack to cool.

Beat together the cream cheese and chocolate hazelnut spread and spread over the top of the cake. Sprinkle over the hazelnuts. Cut into 12 to serve.

AWARENESS POINTS

- Compare the bright green color of the zucchini to the rich orange color of the fruit and eggs. What do you usually associate with the color green? Are you apprehensive about using zucchini in a cake?
- Taste the raw zucchini and note its characteristics—can you spot the same taste once the cake is cooked or is it hidden?
- What is sweeter—the cake base or the cream cheese, hazelnut topping?

White chocolate mousse

Calories per serving 192

Serves 6–8

Preparation time 10 minutes,
  plus chilling

7 oz white chocolate, chopped

4 tablespoons milk

12 cardamom pods

7 oz silken tofu

¼ cup superfine sugar

1 egg white

crème fraîche or plain yogurt, to serve

unsweetened cocoa powder, for dusting

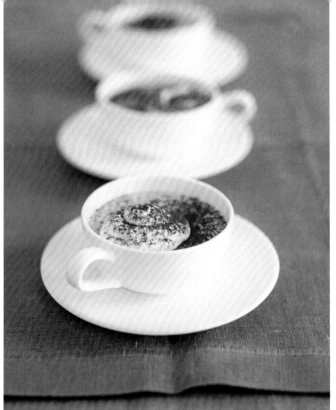

AWARENESS POINTS

- Green cardamom is one of the most expensive spices weight for weight so treat it as a delicacy—handle with care, especially when you release the seeds.
- Appreciate its unique smell. Can you detect the smoky tones?
- When you swallow, notice how the cardamom flavor jumps out of the creamy sweetness.

Put the chocolate and milk in a heatproof bowl and melt over a saucepan of gently simmering water.

To release the cardamom seeds, crush the pods using a mortar and pestle. Discard the pods and crush the seeds finely.

Place the cardamom pods and tofu in a food processor with half of the sugar and blend well to a smooth paste. Turn the mixture into a large bowl.

Whisk the egg white in a thoroughly clean bowl until it forms peaks. Gradually whisk in the remaining sugar.

Beat the melted chocolate mixture into the tofu until completely combined. Using a large metal spoon, fold in the egg white. Spoon the mousse into small coffee cups or glasses and chill for at least 1 hour. Serve topped with spoonfuls of crème fraîche or yogurt and a light dusting of cocoa powder.

Lemon, pistachio & date squares

Calories per square 174 (not including optional chocolate coating)

Makes 15–20

Preparation time 10 minutes, plus cooling and chilling

Cooking time 20 minutes

grated zest of 1 lemon
3 oz ready-to-eat dried dates, chopped
½ cup unsalted pistachios, chopped
¾ cup slivered almonds, chopped
½ cup packed soft light brown sugar
¾ cup millet flakes
1⅓ cups cornflakes, lightly crushed
1 (13 oz) can condensed milk
¼ cup mixed seeds, such as pumpkin and sunflower

Simply place all the ingredients in a large bowl and mix together. Spoon into a 11 x 7 inch baking pan and bake in a preheated oven, 350°F, for 20 minutes.

Remove from the oven and let cool, then mark into 15–20 squares and chill until firm. If you fancy, you could drizzle the top with some melted chocolate once the squares are cooled.

For chocolate & almond squares, make the mixture as above, omitting the pistachios and slivered almonds. Roughly chop ⅔ cup blanched almonds and add to the mixture with 1 cup bran flakes and 2 oz melted semisweet chocolate. Cook and cool, mark and chill as above, drizzling the top with melted white chocolate once cooled, if desired.

AWARENESS POINTS

- Close your eyes, take a pinch from the bowl mixture, and see if you can identify which fruits, seeds, or nut you are eating.
- Can you make out the lemon in the final bake? How does it complement the rich nutty flavor?
- Batch cook these so they can be served to friends, given out at work, or enjoyed as a healthy lunchbox treat.

Guided practice

Desserts are often associated with comfort and warmth. Before you start this recipe, read the text at the start of the chapter and see what food triggers you notice. What has led up to cooking this recipe? Is there an emotional need for soothing? Did a particular memory or thought come to mind? Be kind to yourself, welcome and accept any thoughts as they come to pass.

1 This nourishing dessert is full of taste—cream and butter should be used in moderation, and healthier options used if you prefer. Try to think of it as part of a balanced diet, rather than a guilty pleasure or a reward.

2 Take the time to find different cherries depending on what is in season and available in your grocery store—canned or fresh, you should be able to get an array of colors and sweetness. Before you add the vanilla bean, rub it slightly between your hands and smell the rich aroma. Does the smell of peel and cloves make you feel wintery?

3 As you layer up the dessert to serve, make sure you appreciate all the intricate flavors that have gone in to this dish. Each layer, from the crumble to the cream, should have its own distinct rich taste —distinguish each one with your eye on the spoon; don't just shovel and gulp in one big mush.

4 How does the warmth of the crumble combine with the soothing cool cream? Does the cinnamon bring out a tart flavor in the cherries? Has the fruit juice softened the cookie crumble? Can you make out the sharp fizz of the orange peel?

Cherries with cinnamon crumble

Calories per serving 440
Serves 4–6
Preparation time 15 minutes, plus cooling
Cooking time 20 minutes

3 lb cherries, pitted
1¼ cups superfine sugar
1¾ cups water
1 vanilla bean
2 cloves
strips of orange peel

Crumble
2¼ oz fruit loaf
1 tablespoons unsalted butter
⅛ teaspoon ground cinnamon
1 tablespoon superfine sugar

Cinnamon cream
1 tablespoon confectioners' sugar
⅔ cup whipping cream
¼ teaspoon ground cinnamon

Put the cherries in a large bowl. Place the sugar in a heavy saucepan and add the measured water, vanilla bean, cloves, and orange peel. Bring to a boil, stirring occasionally, then pour the syrup over the cherries. Let cool.

Make the crumble. Cut the fruit loaf into ½ inch dice. Melt the butter and drizzle it over the fruit loaf. Mix together the cinnamon and sugar and sprinkle over the fruit loaf. Mix well, transfer to a baking sheet, and cook in a preheated oven, 375°F, for 4–5 minutes until golden and crunchy. Let cool.

Meanwhile, make the cinnamon cream. Sift the confectioners' sugar over the cream, add the cinnamon, and whisk until firm peaks form.

Serve the cherries with a small amount of syrup, a spoonful of the cinnamon cream, and a sprinkling of the fruit loaf crumble. Decorate with the strips of orange peel.

Moist banana & carrot cake

Calories per serving 183

Serves 14 slices

Preparation time 10 minutes,
  plus cooling

Cooking time 1 hour 40 minutes

butter, for greasing
1 cup ready-to-eat dried apricots,
  coarsely chopped
½ cup water
1 egg
2 tablespoons honey
1 cup walnuts, roughly chopped
1 lb ripe bananas, mashed
1 large carrot, about 4 oz, shredded
1¾ cups all-purpose flour, sifted
1 teaspoon baking powder

Topping
⅔ cup cream cheese
2 tablespoons lemon curd

AWARENESS POINTS
- Shop around for different types of honey—you'll find a huge range of flavors.
- Take the time to appreciate how amazing the natural process of bees making honey is.
- What flavor is strongest—the apricot, the banana, or the lemon? Would you adjust the recipe next time?

Grease a 2 lb loaf pan and line with nonstick parchment paper. Place the apricots in a small saucepan with the measured water, bring to a boil, and simmer for 10 minutes. Transfer to a blender or food processor and blend to a thick puree.

Put all the other cake ingredients in a large bowl and add the apricot puree. Mix well, then spoon into the prepared pan.

Bake in a preheated oven, 350°F, for 1½ hours or until a skewer inserted in the center comes out clean. Turn out onto a wire rack to cool.

Beat together the cream cheese and lemon curd and spread over the top of the loaf.

Chocolate sorbet

Calories per serving 295

Serves 6–8

Makes about 900 ml (1½ pints)

Preparation time 15 minutes,
   plus chilling and freezing

Cooking time 10 minutes

2½ cups water

⅔ cup packed soft dark brown sugar

1 cup granulated sugar

½ cup unsweetened cocoa powder

1 oz semisweet chocolate with 70%
   cocoa solids, finely chopped

2½ teaspoons vanilla extract

1 teaspoon instant espresso
   coffee powder

Put the measured water, sugars, and cocoa powder in a saucepan and mix together. Heat gently, stirring until the sugar has dissolved. Increase the heat to bring the mixture to a boil, then reduce to a simmer for 8 minutes.

Remove the pan from the heat and stir in the chocolate, vanilla extract, and espresso powder until thoroughly dissolved. Pour into a bowl and cool over ice or let cool and chill.

Freeze in an ice-cream machine according to the manufacturer's directions. Serve immediately or transfer to a chilled plastic freezerproof container and store in the freezer for up to 1 month. If you are using the sorbet straight from the freezer, transfer to the refrigerator 20 minutes before serving to soften slightly.

AWARENESS POINTS

- See if you can learn to love the natural taste of unsweetened chocolate.
- Does the espresso smell trigger anything? Does it make you feel enlivened?
- Add a small scoop of sorbet to different fresh fruit throughout the week for a healthy treat.

Ricotta & maple syrup cheesecake

Calories per serving 375

Serves 8

Preparation time 20 minutes,
   plus chilling

3 gelatin leaves
4 oz graham crackers, crushed
3½ tablespoons reduced-fat sunflower
   spread, melted
scant 1 cup cottage cheese
scant 1 cup ricotta cheese
2 egg whites
¼ cup sifted confectioners' sugar
2 tablespoons lemon juice
scant ¼ cup water
4 tablespoons maple syrup

To decorate
2 oranges, peeled and sliced
sprigs of red currants

Line an 8 inch springform pan with nonstick parchment paper. Soften the gelatin in cold water.

Mix together the cracker crumbs and melted sunflower spread and press into the prepared pan. Refrigerate.

Strain together the cottage cheese and ricotta. Whisk the egg whites in a thoroughly clean bowl until stiffly peaking, then beat in the confectioners' sugar until glossy.

Put the lemon juice and measured water in a saucepan over low heat and stir in the gelatin until dissolved. Add to the ricotta mix with the maple syrup, then fold in the egg whites. Pour the mixture over the cracker base and refrigerate until set.

Decorate with the sliced oranges and sprigs of red currants before serving.

AWARENESS POINTS

- If you like to know the science behind what you are cooking, then this is a recipe for you. There are plenty of ingredients that change from solid to liquid state and vice versa in this method—maybe do some reading to discover why.
- Watch the gelatin soften—what do you know about its molecular structure?
- Enjoy the feel of the cracker crumbling between your fingers—don't be afraid to get messy. Think about the surface area of the bread crumbs.

The one-month eating plan

Kindly remember that this is an invitation to relearn the joy of eating well and giving up an unnecessary struggle.

Week one:

- **Five days (or more)** start a mindful eating practice as explained on page 19. Initially it might be best to choose a short meal to eat on your own.

- **Use a notebook** and write down what you felt when eating mindfully.

- **Ask yourself:**
  Am I really hungry? Starving/ hungry/ slightly hungry/ not really hungry?
  Is my portion size appropriate for my hunger? Yes/No?
  Is it food I really want or other forms of nourishment, e.g. relaxation?

- **Five days a week** practice the Body Scan exercise (see page 14).

- **At least five times a week** engage in an everyday informal mindfulness practice (e.g. mindful shower, mindful tooth brushing, etc.)

Week two:

- **Continue with a mindful eating practice** (as in week one) five times a week—now try a main meal even if you only manage three spoonfuls. Again use your notebook as before.

- **Do a mindful movement practice** (e.g. mindful walking, mindful swimming) five times a week

- **Two days a week practice** the Body Scan exercise (see page 14).

Week three:

- **Continue with a mindful eating practice** (as in week one) five times a week—now try a main meal with others (see page 88). Again use your notebook as before.

- **Exercise:** Do the breath awareness practice for 5–10 minutes (see pages 32–3). Do a mindful movement practice (e.g. mindful walking, mindful swimming) five times a week

- **Two days a week** practice the Body Scan exercise (see page 14).

Week four:

- **Continue with a mindful eating practice** (as in week one) five times a week. Also focus on "finding your triggers" (see pages 22–30). Again use your notebook as before.

- **Do a mindful movement** practice five times a week.

- **Alternate Body Scan** or a breath exercise five times a week.

- **Try something new every day ...**

And now ...

Do a selection from the above for the rest of your life.

Weekly eating planner

This meal plan offers a few suggestions of what to eat for the first week of eating mindfully. For the following weeks, try to listen to your body's signals and choose your own recipes accordingly.

Monday

BREAKFAST: Very berry fromage frais fool | PAGE 52

LUNCH: Chicken minestrone | PAGE 67

DINNER: Lentil moussaka | PAGE 107

Tuesday

BREAKFAST: Granola squares | PAGE 55

LUNCH: Beet, spinach & orange salad | PAGE 74

DINNER: Burmese chicken noodle curry | PAGE 114

Wednesday

BREAKFAST: Oatmeal with prune compote | PAGE 41

LUNCH: Aromatic chicken packages | PAGE 76

DINNER: Seafood & vegetable stir-fry | PAGE 112

Thursday

BREAKFAST: Figs with honey & yogurt | PAGE 58

LUNCH: Greek country salad with halloumi | PAGE 78

DINNER: Salmon curry with tomato salad | PAGE 106

Friday

BREAKFAST: Cranberry muffins | PAGE 43

LUNCH: Seared chicken sandwich | PAGE 80

DINNER: Quick prosciutto & arugula pizza | PAGE 94

Saturday

BREAKFAST: Moroccan baked eggs | PAGE 49

LUNCH: Salmon & bulgur wheat pilaf | PAGE 63

DINNER: Lamb stuffed with rice & peppers | PAGE 89

Sunday

BREAKFAST: Banana & golden raisin drop scones | PAGE 47

LUNCH: Roast pork & fennel | PAGE 95

DINNER: Squash, kale & mixed bean soup | PAGE 105

Index

Acknowledgments

The Mindfulness Cookbook Picture Acknowledgments

Recipe photography © Octopus Publishing Group

Additional photography:
Alamy moodboard 116; PhotoAlto sas 12. Getty Images Fuse 84; Guido Mieth 58; Joshua Hodge Photography 28; Michael H 8; Ryan McVay 36; T-Pool/STOCK4B 30.